SCHOOL, COMMUNITY AND THE STATE

Edited by

PROFESSOR SACHCHIDANANDA

Hony. Director

Sulabh Institute of Development Studies, Patna

and

Chairman

A.N. Sinha Institute of Scoail Studies, Patna

SERIALS PUBLICATIONS

New Delhi

First Published—2005

ISBN : 81-86771-63-8

Published by

Head Office : **SERIALS PUBLICATIONS**
4, B.S.S. Hall, Khyber Pass Market,
Civil Lines, Delhi-110054 (India)
Fax: 91-11-23812678
Phone : 23245225
e-mail : serials@satyam.net.in

Branch Office : 4830/24, Prahlad Street, Ansari Road,
Darya Ganj, New Delhi-110002 (India)

PREFACE

With the establishment of Sulabh Institute of Development Studies in July 1996 we started taking up research projects sponsored by many government and semi-government organizations on different aspects of socioeconomic activities. Besides taking up the social cause of scavengers, their identification, liberation and rehabilitation, our main focus was on the Sociology of Education. Our most important concern has been to explore the interface between school, community and the State. In recent decades them in deep concern over people's participation in the entire educational process since it has been felt that government agencies alone can not succeed in meeting the Constitutional commitment over universalization of elementary education. We took up research projects sponsored by **State Institute of Educational Management and Training (SIEMAT)**, Patna, **SIEMAT**, Allahabad, The Bihar Education Project, **National Institute of Open Schooling (NIOS)**, etc. In course of time study reports were submitted to the sponsoring agencies. However, our findings, which we consider important, were only shared with the sponsoring authorities. Concerned scholars had no idea of our findings.

Under these circumstances, we thought it advisable to compile these findings in the form of self contained articles followed by an overview and select bibliography. It is with this purpose that we approach the readers with our findings on a platter. Those who are interested in going into greater detail may contact the **Sulabh Institute of Development Studies (SIDS)** since most of the research reports are unpublished. Four papers have been contributed by Dr. Niraj Kumar and four others by Dr. Rajkumar Pandey, both Research Officers at the institute. The first and the last paper have been contributed by me. Although not based on field work they throw some light on allied aspects of U.E.E.

I am grateful to Shri S. K. Jha of the Serials Publications for having agreed to bring out this volume.

Sachchidananda
Editor

CONTENTS

THE CONTRIBUTORS

Professor Sachchidananda, currently Chairman at the A. N. Sinha Institute of Social Studies, Patna, has been a pioneer in the field of Anthropological studies in Bihar. He was educated in the Patna University and the School of Oriental and African Studies, University of London, founder of Post Graduate Department of Anthropology at Ranchi. He was later Director of the Tribal Research Institute, Ranchi and of the A. N. Sinha Institute of Social Studies at Patna. He was also the Vice-Chancellor of Ranchi University. His wide ranging research interests cover culture change in tribal areas, shifting cultivation, social dimensions of agriculture development, Harijan educated elite, women's rights, educational problems of the disadvantaged sections of the population, voluntary action in tribal areas and socio-cultural dimensions of development. He has contributed a large number of papers to research journals in India and aboard and published twenty five books in Sociology and Anthropology. He has also edited the four volume 'Profile of Indian Tribes (1995).' A past President of the Anthropology Section of Indian Science Congress, he is also the recipient of R. P. Chanda and S.C. Roy Medals for distinguished work in Anthropology from the Asiatic Society of Bengal.

Raj Kumar Pandey has a doctorate in Economics from Patna University. He received training in Block/Micro level planning from **AVARD**, New Delhi and PRA in Project Management from **PRAXIS (Action Aid)**. He has worked in Indian Statistical Institute, Kolkata, A. N. Sinha Institute of Social Studies, Patna. His areas of interest are sustainable development, empowerment of deprived groups, problem of manual scavenging and water supply and sanitation in rural areas. Currently he is a Senior Research Officer at the Sulabh Institute of Development Studies, Patna.

Niraj Kumar holds a Doctorate in Sociology from Institute of Social Sciences, Agra. His area of interest is Sociology of Education and has completed about half dozen research projects in this area. He has in his credit few research papers and a book. At present he is working as a Research Officer at Sulabh Institute of Development Studies, Patna.

1

PRIMARY EDUCATION IN INDIA AT THE THRESHOLD OF THE NEW MILLENIUM

SACHCHIDANANDA

1. Why Primary Education

Most of the developing countries in the world are addressing the challenge of Education For All. It has been universally recognized that to meet the development goals aimed at eradicating extreme poverty and improving the quality of life of the people, education is one of the most powerful instruments for reducing poverty and inequality and paving the way for sustained economic growth. It is also a necessary condition for the existence of democratic societies. Both for the individual and nation education is the key to creation, application and spread of knowledge. It is this commitment to achieve universal primary education by the year 2000 was made by a large number of countries in Jomtein in Thailand in 1990. This commitment was reaffirmed and extended at the World Education Forum in Dakar in 2000.

The development goals were identified and the target dates were fixed for their achievement. The goals included eradication of extreme poverty and hunger, achievement of universal primary education promotion of gender equality and empowerment of women, reduction in child mortality and improvement of maternal health, combating HIV/AIDS and other diseases, ensuring environmental sustainability and development of global partnership for development. The Dakar declaration stressed that all boys and girls in different countries should be able to complete full course of primary schooling by 2015. It also wanted to eliminate gender disparity in primary education by 2005. However, it was also realized that achievement of the goals by the dates fixed was not possible in all countries. Experience shows that the dates have to be extended from time to time in many countries. Efforts were also made to analyze the reasons for not achieving the target in many countries.

In this gigantic effort, achievements of goals in primary education has the top priority. Primary education develops the capacity to learn, read and use mathematics, to acquire information and to think critically about information. Primary education is also the gateway to higher level of education. Micro-economic research has revealed that education improves individual income. Research also indicates the contribution of primary education to better natural resource management and more rapid technological adaptation and innovation. When a large share of children do not complete primary education the productivity of the labour force and the human potential from which the society and economy can draw, are limited. In several developing regions the average level of schooling of the labour force is still less than a complete primary education. Researches in this area have brought out that such low level of human capital is fundamentally inadequate for sustained development and poverty reduction. It has also been pointed out that without six years of schooling the development goals can not be achieved. The role of primary education in reducing poverty and inequality has been strongly established. Illiteracy is one of the strongest predictors of poverty and inequal access to educational opportunity is one of the correlates of income inequality.

It is clearly visible in societies in respect to poor girls, ethnic minorities, orphans, people with disabilities and people living in rural areas. Extending adequate quality primary education to these vulnerable groups is crucial to equip them to contribute to and benefit from economic growth. The International Literacy Survey reveals high correlation between country level of income inequality and inequality in the distribution of literacy.

Ultimately the case for universal primary education goes beyond economic consideration. Nobel laureate Amratya Sen has called for human capabilities - the essential and individual power to reflect, make better choice, seek a voice and enjoy a better life. Primary education promotes the achievement of all the Millenium development goals. Education for girls is one of the strongest movers of improvement in fertility, health and nutritional outcomes. Its impact is also felt on infant and child mortality and enhanced family welfare. It has been found that mothers who have completed primary education are 50% more likely to ensure that their infants are immunized than others with no education. Research data also indicates that for boys and girls education may be the single most effective weapon against HIV/AIDS. However, primary education completion should not be regarded as terminal education. It is only the first step towards the ultimate goal of life long learning. This is as much relevant for the poorest countries of the developing world as it is for countries of the Organization for Economic Co-operation and Development (OECD). In the highly compatitive economy no country can any longer consider primary schooling a terminal level of education for its labour force.

A large number of researches suggests that completion of atleast five to six years of schooling is a critical threshold for sustainable mastery of basic competencies, such as, literacy and numeracy. In less than five to six years of schooling children remain functionally illiterate for the rest of their lives. This has serious implication from a human capital perspective. There is a substantial difference between getting all children enrolled in primary school and ensuring that they complete five years primary education. There are substantial disparities between gross enrolment ratio and the primary completion rate. There are many reasons for this. Sometime children enter school below the official schooling age or more commonly in the developing countries they start school late. They may repeat grades. Children dropout because of their own or family member's illness or to meet the needs of the family labour force. Important gender differences also exist in the school completion rates. In countries like India where education for girls is a low priority in rural areas, the percentage of drop out among girl children is larger than among boys. It is also interesting to note that among the lowest income quatile the drop out rate is very high. In India among several sections of the population, such as scheduled castes and tribes there is a dramatic disparity in the school completion rate on account of heavy dropouts, largely on account of economic reasons.

We assume that given all facilities every child can learn. If this does not happen the onus is on the school system to prepare teachers with diverse pedagogical strategy to meet children's diverse learning needs. The school system has to allocate resources so that special support is provided to slow learners, children with physical or emotional disabilities or children who can not attend school regularly on account of poverty. The school system has to devise methods of learning assessment to ensure that children grade progression actually reflects mastery of primary curriculum.

2. The Indian Scenario

17% of the world's population lives in India which comprises 2.4% of the world's area. Since independence the country has witnessed phenomenal educational development both in quantitative and qualitative terms.

But the national goals of Universal elementary education and the total eradication of illiteracy have still remained elusive. The Government is committed to achieve this national goal and has been steadily increasing the budget allocation for education. India spent 4.02% of its GDP on education during 2001-2002 but about 44% of its adult population is still outside the educational net. In China the percentage of adult illiterate population is only 15% and it spends 2.3% of its GNP on education. Thailand whose illiterate population percentage is the same as India spends 4.8% of its GNP on education.

A look at the table below reveals an irregular rise and fall in the percentage of expenditure on education from 1951-52 to 2001 - 2002. There has been an annual average growth of 0.11% during the period under review.

Table 1 : Public expenditure on education in India

Year	%of Education Expenditure to GDP
1951-52	0.64
1961-62	1.52
1971-72	2.25
1981-82	2.92
1990-91	3.84
1991-92	3.80
1992-93	3.72
1993-94	3.62
1994-95	3.56
1995-96	3.56
1996-97	3.53
1997-98	3.49
1998-99	3.85
1999-2000	4.25
2000-2001	4.30
2001-2002	4.02

The expenditure on elementary education was 1.78% of the GDP in 1990-91. This shows a gradual fall to 1.65% in 1994-95 and then a gradual rise to 2.02% in 2001-2002. The share of expenditure on elementary education to total education in all sectors was 6.19% during 1990. This shows an irregular rise and fall and finally settled at 6.61% during 2001-02. The per capita budgeted expenditure during this year was lowest in Bihar followed by Uttar Pradesh and Orissa.

There has been a considerable increase in the number of education institutions, during this period. The number of primary schools increased 33 times. The number of Upper primary schools increased 16 times.

Table 2 : Growth of primary and upper primary schools from 1950-51 to 2001-2002

Year	Primary	Upper Primary
1950-51	209671	13596
1960-61	330399	49663
1970-71	408378	90621
1980-81	494503	118555
1990-91	560935	151456
2000-01	638738	206269
2001-02	664041	219626

Both primary and upper primary schools are managed by different organizations such as the government, government and local bodies. Besides these a small percentage of private aided and private unaided institutions, exist.

There has been steady growth in school enrolment at different levels between 1950-51 to 2001 - 2002. The total enrolment at the primary and upper primary level increased by 6 and 14 times respectively. The girls enrolment increased by 9.37 and 60 times respectively. This is evident from the table below:

Table 3: Percentage of girls enrolment to total enrolment

Year	Primary (I - V)		
	Boys	Girls	Total
1950-51	13.8	5.4	19.2
1960-61	23.6	11.4	35.0
1970-71	35.7	21.3	57.0
1980-81	45.3	28.5	73.8
1990-91	57.0	40.4	97.4
2000-01	64.0	49.8	113.8
2001-02	63.6	50.3	113.9

The participation of girls has been increasing steadily since 1950-51. Girls, participation has increased manifold in the primary sector.

Table 4 : Percentage of girls enrolment to total enrolment

Year	Primary (I - V)
1950-51	28.1
1960-61	32.6
1970-71	37.4
1980-81	38.6
1990-91	41.5
2000-01	43.7
2001-02	44.1

The number of girls, enrolment per hundred boys enrolled is indicated in the following table 5. The enrolment has increased from 39 to 79 in primary classes.

Table 5 : Number of girls enrolment per hundred boys enrolled

Year	Primary (I - V)
1950-51	39
1960-61	48
1970-71	60
1980-81	63
1990-91	71
2000-01	78
2001-02	79

The total scheduled caste enrolment at the primary and upper primary School from 1980-81 to 2001 - 2002 is given below: The scheduled caste girls, enrolment increased 2.5 times.

Table 6 : Enrolment of scheduled caste students in primary schools

Year	Primary (I - V)		
	Boys	Girls	Total
1980-81	7213	3768	10981
1990-91	9737	6057	15794
2000-01	12059	9136	21195
2001-02	12251	9253	21504

The total ST enrolment at the primary stage increased 2.5 times. The ST girls, enrolment increased by 3.3 times. This is evident from table given below :

Table 7 : Enrolment of scheduled tribes students in primary

Year	Primary (I - V)		
	Boys	Girls	Total
1980-81	3133	1527	4660
1990-91	4958	2911	7869
2000-01	6330	4665	10995
2001-02	6691	5040	11731

There has been substantial increase in the number of teachers since 1950-51 in all types of schools. The total number of teachers in primary schools increased from 5.38 lacs in 1950-51 to 19.28 lacs in 2001-2002. The number of female teachers increased from 0.82 lacs in 1950-51 to 7.15 lacs in 2001-2002 that is by about 8 times as is evident from the table below.

Table 8 : Teachers in primary schools

Year	Male	Female	Total
1950-51	456	82	538
1960-61	615	127	742
1970-71	835	225	1060
19 80-81	1021	342	1363
1990-91	1143	473	1616
2000-01	1221	675	1896

The Gross Enrolment Ratio (GER) is defined as the percentage of enrolment in primary classes in the estimated child population in the age group 6 to 11.

Table 9 : Gross enrolment ratio

Year	Boys	Girls	Total
1950-51	60.6	24.8	42.6
1960-61	82.6	41.4	62.4
1970-71	95.5	60.5	78.6
1980-81	95.8	64.1	80.5
1990-91	114.0	85.5	100.1
2000-01	104.9	85.9	95.7
2001-02	105.3	86.9	96.3

Since 1950-51 we see a gradual increase in the trend of gross enrolment ratio at the national level among both boys and girls at the primary level. This is an area where our effort to enroll maximum school going age children in school has proved fruitful.

Table 10 : Gross enrolment ratio of schedule caste students

Year	Primary (I - V) (6-11age group)		
	Boys	Girls	Total
1986-87	103.8	64.8	84.8
1991-92	121.4	83.5	102.9
1995-96	109.9	83.2	97.1
1999-00	103.6	80.5	92.4
2000-01	107.3	85.8	96.8
2001-02	103.1	82.3	93.0

Note : Enrolment in this stage includes underage and overage children. Hence the total percentage may be over hundred in some cases.

Changes in the agrarian economy, new occupational opportunities as well as adult franchise have given some leverage to scheduled caste communities to defy traditional social norms and taboos. Many parts of India are witness to socio-political mobilization of scheduled castes who are increasingly demanding their right. One of the critical factors for their economic betterment in the post independence period has been formal education as is evident from their satisfactory gross enrolment ratio.

The Gross Enrolment ratio of ST children in age group of 6 - 11 is given below :

Table 11 : Gross enrolment ratio (GER) of Schedule tribe students

Year	Primary (I - V)		
	Boys	Girls	Total
1986-87	111.0	68.0	90.1
1991-92	125.6	82.6	104.7
1995-96	115.0	80.2	96.9
1999-00	112.7	82.7	97.7
2000 -01	116.9	85.5	101.1
2001-02	106.9	85.1	96.3

In a highly stratified society like India, there are numerous layers of differentiation apart from caste and class. Gender is now recognized as a more pervasive and distinct category of social stratification. In the context of literacy, gender is an important aspect. The enrolment ratio among tribal girls is not only low but shows a high level of gender disparity.

The Gender parity index is calculated by dividing girls GER by Boys GER of a given level of education. It measures progress towards gender equity in education when the GPI shows value equal to one, it shows that there is no gender disparity at that level and learning opportunity is available to girls is equal to that for boys. The table below indicates the gradual rise in gender parity in primary education. It has increased from 0.41 in 1950-51 to 0.83 in 2001 - 2002, as is evident from the table below :

Table 12 : Gender parity index of students

Year	Boys
1950-51	0.41
1960-61	051
1970-71	0.63
1980-81	0.67
1990-91	0.75
2000 - 01	0.82
2001-02	0.83

The gross drop out rates represent the percentage of people about drop out from a given grade or a level of education in a given school year. The data reveals that there has been a fall in the dropout rate from 64.9% in 1960-61 to 39% in 2001 to 2002 at the primary school level.

Table 13 : Gross drop-out rates

Year	Boys	Girls	Total
1960-61	61.7	70.9	64 9
1970-71	64.5	70.9	67 0
1980-81	56.2	62.5	58.7
1990-91	40.1	46.0	42.6
1992-93	43.8	46.7	45.0
1999-2000	38.7	42.3	40.3
2001-02	38.4	39.0	39.0

On the basis of the number of female and male teachers the number of female teachers per hundred male teachers in primary schools is given table 14 : The number of female teachers has increased 3 times at the primary level. This shows a larger participation of women in education and development.

Table 14 : Number of Female teaches per 100 male teachers in primary schools

Year	Boys
1950-51	20
1960-61	21
1970-71	27
1980-81	33
1990-91	41
2000 - 01	55
2001-02	59

On the basis of school enrolment and the number of teachers, the pupil-teacher ratio from 1950-51 to 2001 - 2002 at the primary level during the year 1950-51 was 1:24. This ratio has now increased 1:43 in primary schools. Though the number of educational institutions has considerably increased, the higher PTR indicates that utilization of educational facilities have also increased. The increased enrolment at various levels also scores the need for opening of greater number of educational institutions and improving the quality of education. The PTR from 1950-51 to 2001 - 02 at the primary level is given below :

Table 15 : Pupil - Teacher ratio

Year	Boys
1950-51	24
1960-61	36
1970-71	39
1980-81	38
1990-91	43
2000 - 01	43
2001 - 02	43

3. Initiatives And Interventions

In the Indian Constitution school education was included in the State list. As such, it was responsibility of the State government to provide universalization of elementary education. At the policy level the situation changed with Constitutional change made in 1976 by which school education was put in the concurrent list. U.E.E. became a shared responsibility of the Central and State government. The national government realised its direct responsibility in this field after the adoption of National Policy of education in 1986. In the 1990s there was very intensive activity in the field of literacy in elementary education. Issues of adult literacy in elementary education and its direct relationship to development entered public discourse. This led the Union government to procure and channilise funds from international agencies for initiatives and interventions in a big way in different States. The stress in recent decades is now to sustain and deepen current reforms in elementary education with the help of local planning and new management strategies.

It is recognized that growth in elementary education is largely determined by State specific conditions. Mere funds and schemes from the centre will not guarantee the achievement of U.E.E. goal. It is very much dependent on the tradition and values of local communities, commitment and enthusiasm of State level educational leadership, political will of the State government and the capacity to adopt innovative approaches. It is on account of these factors that differential success has been achieved in different States.

To reduce the impact of rising cost of textbooks and exercise books the government has exempted writing and printing paper supplied to all the State Texbook Corporation from excise duty. This would enhance the affordability of text books for the disadvantaged section of the society.

On account of the spread of Total Literacy Campaign environment building for primary education has accelerated massive community mobilization. There is now a demand for education as one of the primary needs even among families in which there was no education earlier.

Under the Kasturba Gandhi Siksha Yojana a large number of residential schools for girls has been established in all districts which have low level of female literacy. In addition to this, the Central Government has also decided to grant financial incentive for the girl child belonging to families below the poverty line.

Most of the State and Central Governments have introduced projects to address the objectives and the strategies of National Policy on Education 1986. Special attention has been paid to increase community involvement , improving teaching and learning materials and providing inservice teacher's training for better performance.

One of the earliest such schemes known as Operation Blackboard was started in 1987. It is aimed at improving the school climate and enhancing retention and learning achievement of children by providing certain minimum essential facilities in all primary schools. The scheme has brought about remarkable qualitative and quantitative improvement in primary education. More than 523000 primary schools have already been started all over the country under this scheme.

Decentralised planning and management of elementary education visualise direct community involvement in the form of Village Education Committees. The action plan uses micro-planning as a tool for designing a family-wise and child-wise plan by which every child regularly attends the school or the NFE centres, continues his education in a nearby place and completes atleast eight years of schooling on its equivalent at NFE centre.

Through the introduction of Panchayati Raj which aims at the transfer of power to the people, the participation of local institutions of self government has been ensured. The Panchayati Raj institutions have to play a more dynamic and proactive role in education.

These structures have provided voice to women, scheduled castes and tribes, minorities, parents and educational functionaries. Panchayati Raj bodies have been delegated the responsibility of the supervision of entire educational process in their areas. They can choose the locations of the schools on the basis of micro-planning and school mapping. The decentralization of school management to grass-root level bodies is an important policy initiative.

During the Eighth plan the District Primary Education Plan shifted the planning mechanism from the State to the district level. Lok Jumbish, one such initiative in Rajsthan has gone one step further by assigning decision making process to a block level committee. At the village level the VEC is mainly responsible for community mobilisation, school mapping, renovation and construction of school building and improvement in school curriculum. The VEC of the Siksha Karmi schools have been activated as a result of the Lok Junbish effort.

On 15th August, 1995, the School Meal Programme was started to increase enrolment, retention and attendance in primary classes by providing supplementary nutrition to all children in primary schools. The scheme has spread throughout the country. Hundred grams of food grains in the form of cooked meal is given to every child per school day in classes I to V. By 1997-98, 110 million children in primary classes were covered under this scheme. Evaluation reports have confirmed the positive impact on students enrolment and retention.

District Primary Education Programme (DPEP)

This programme was launched in November 1994 with a view to overhauling the primary education system. The programme aims at translating into action the strategies for achieving U.E.E. through the district specific planning and disaggregated target setting. It draws upon the cumulative experience of several State level initiatives started earlier. It makes a shift from the schematic piece-meal approach of the earlier programmes to a holistic view of primary education with emphasis on decentralized planning and community mobilization with district specific planning based on local conditions. The basic objectives of DPEP are :

1. To provide all children access to primary education through either the formal or non-formal stream.
2. To reduce differences in enrolment, drop-out rates and learning achievement among gender and weaker section groups to less than five percent.
3. To reduce overall primary dropout rates for all children to less than 10%.
4. To rase the average achievement rate by 25% by measured baseline level and ensuring achievement of basic literacy and numeracy competencies and minimum of 40% achievement in other competencies by all primary education children.

The Government of India finances 85% of the project cost as a grant to DPEP State implementation bodies. The rest of the cost is met by the State government. The bulk of the funds for DPEP come from international bodies such as the UNICEF, European Union, ODA (U.K.), SIDA (Sweden), Netherlands etc. The first phase of the progrmame was launched in 42 districts in the States of Assam, Haryana, Karnataka, Kerala, Maharashtra, Tamil Nadu and Madhya Pradesh. Later the programme was launched in 80 districts of Orissa, Himachal Pradesh, Andhra Pradesh, Uttar Pradesh, West Bengal and Gujarat. The impact studies of the first phase projects are very positive. The DPEP has made decisive impact on increasing enrolment, reducing stagnation and improving class-room transaction.

While the DPEP has been operational in backward districts with female literacy below the national average,

TLC has stepped up the demand for elementary education.

Bihar Education Project

The project was started in 1991 to bring about quantitative and qualitative improvement in elementary education. The emphasis is on education of the deprived section, of the community such as SC, ST and women. Participatory planning and implementation are the crucial ingredients of the programme. The main achievement of the project are :

(a) Building up a strong Mahila Samakhya Component

The Mahila Samakhya starts from the presumption that education can make a decisive intervention towards the equality of women in society. Education has to be more than classroom exercise. Education is not perceived as a priority need both by women and the society at large. The daily struggle for food, fuel and water keeps her bogged down. She has little say in decision making in her own home or society in general. She has little control over her body and her life. This results in very low self image and lack of confidence. The Mahila Samakhya seeks to address itself to these constraints. The new women has to break away from a state of positive expectation of her condition and move toward a situation where she can articulate her need, speak her mind and participate with confidence and share her responsibilities. The Samakhya approach starts with the identification of collective strength. It seeks to create an environment where women demand knowledge and information which empowers them to play a positive role in their own development and development of society. It seeks to work through informal educational structures which respect women pace and rythm of learning, given the multiple demand of the household and changing agricultural seasons. The Samakhya would create a cadre of aware and educated rural women thereby promoting in rural areas an environment supportive to the goals of this project.

(b) Organization of VECs and Community involvement in programme implementation at the grass-root level.

(c) Non-formal education through NGOs.

The project has completed two phases by 1998. It is still running. It is proposed to merge the project with DPEP.

Uttar Pradesh Basic Education Programme

The project for Education For All was prepared by government of U. P. and started working in 1993. It was initially in operation in 12 districts but in second phase expanded to 15 more districts. The construction work of schools and Block Resource Centres have been completed as per schedule. Training materials for teacher trainers in DIETs have been prepaired. Continuous training of teachers have been going on.

Andhra Pradesh Primary Education Project

This project was started in districts with female literacy of just 34%. It has adopted a two step strategy of improving class-room transaction by training teachers and promoting school construction activities. More than 80,000 teachers have been trained in all districts and more than 3,000 training centres became operational.

Shiksha Karmi and Lok Jambish Project

In Rajasthan the Siksha Karmi project was started in 1987 with assistance from Sweedish International Development Agency. The project aims at universalization and qualitative improvement of education in the remote and socio- economically backward villages of the State with primary focus on girls. To off-set the problems of teacher absenteeism, the project used an alternative strategy by recruiting local youths known as Siksha Karmis in schools. They have been provided with training and supervisory support. The mobilization and participation of the community in the functioning of primary schools is an important feature of this project. The School Karmi project also runs non-formal classes. The project is known for its open participative style to achieve its objectives. The approach, strategies and achievement of the SKP has attracted national and international recognition.

Another project called the Lok Jumbish project has made a profound impression on the primary education scenario in Rajasthan. The project covers 75 blocks with a total population of 12 millions. It has helped in brining together government agencies, teachers, NGOs, elected representatives and people into an interactive group to promote universalization of primary education. The guiding principles of Lok Jumbish are that it is a process rather than a product, partnership, decentralized functioning, participatory functioning, integration with main education system and creating multiple levels of leadership committed to quality and mission mode.

Special attention has been given to environment building in all its programmes. This helps in understanding the issues involved in people's mobilization. In both these projects mobilising village community has ensured quality education for every child. Community involvement is the key factor for the success of the two projects. Lok Jumbish has a positive effect on the empowerment of the locally elected people especially the women representative at village level who are often the active members of its core team. The VEC members are trained through environment building and are actively involved in school matters. The SKP has constituted VEC in 2000 villages to promote community involvement and encourage village level planning. The role of VEC is to mobilise resources for construction of schools and for infrastructure. It also helps in framing the school calendars and deciding about school timings. The two projects have demonstrated how the deeply rooted problems of primary education in rural India can be addressed. Wide dissemination of them innovative projects can inspire other projects all over India.

In recent decades Himachal Pradesh has experienced a remarkable education break through. In terms of rural literacy rate Himachal ranked second in literacy among sixteen major States. For the first time this achievement was hailed by the PROBE survey in 1999. The overall literacy rate in the State jumped from 21.26% in 1961 to 77.13% in 2001. The difference between male and female literacy rate has also gone down effectively over these years. There are many factors which explain this outstanding achievement. The hill society is more egalitarian and caste distinctions are less oppressive than in the plains. The Himachali women have a unique place in the society. The fruits of education have also promoted public motivation for schooling. The spread of education was facilitated by the focus on construction of roads. The first Chief Minister of the State is credited with creating a momentum that established the precedence of primary education on the agenda of the political elites of the State. Primary education remained a priority of the State government, which ever party was in power. This sustained commitment to school has enabled the State to overcome its initial education disadvantage.

Special schemes like Operation Blackboard was taken seriously by the State government which had its own schemes for physical education, the V.T. (Voluntary Teacher System) and the flexible planning about agriculture calendar and climatic conditions. This is accompanied by expansion of job opportunities.

The Mahila Mandals have been very active. Himachali women are more confident and assertive. This is on account of their deep involvement in the struggle for survival. Their contribution to labour force is more than in the three neighbouring States. The motivation for girl education is very high. The demand for girl education has increased as educated boys prefer educated women as their mates. Education is seen as important for girls as it helps them in domestic duties and in looking after the children. Education opens the door for many opportunities. Growth in education has been accelerated on account of community involvement and community support. Since the school system is functional and parents are gaining from it, they are willing to contribute to the schooling facilities and to see that schools are not closed arbitrarily. There is very good rapport between parents and teachers. Education is seen as a tool for establishing equity in society. Education of the child has become a societal norm. It has also been realized that adult literacy programmes may solve the problem of literacy but they can not be a substitute for a good schooling system.

Sarva Siksha Abhiyan (S.S.A.)

The SSA is a flagship programme of the national government in the new millenium. It seeks to achieve the goal of universal primary education by 2005 and the goal of UEE by 2010. This would mean that children in all States would complete atleast five years of schooling or its equivalent through the non-formal means by the year 2005. SSA is an effort to universalize elementary education by community ownership of the school system. It is a response to the demand for quality basic education all over the country. It is also an attempt to provide an opportunity for improving human capabilities to all children through provision of community owned quality education in a mission mode.

Meaning of Sarva Shiksha Abhiyan :

(a) A programme for clear time frame for universal elementary education.

(b) A response to the demand for quality basic education all over the country.

(c) An opportunity for promoting social justice through basic education.

(d) An effort at effectively involving the Pnchayati Raj Institutions, School Management Committees, Village and Urban Slum Level Education Committees, Parent's Teacher's Associations, Mother Teacher Associations, Tribal Autonomous Councils and other grass root level structures in the management of elementary schools.

(e) An expression of political will for universal elementary education across the country.

(f) A partnership between the central, State and the local government .

(g) An opportunity for States to develop their own vision of elementary education.

Aims of SSA

The SSA seeks to provide useful and relevant elementary education to all children in six to fourteen age group by 2010. Its other goal is to bridge social, regional and gender gaps with the active participation of the community in the management of schools. It is a quest for an education system that does not alienate the child from the society and seeks to promote community solidarity. The children are allowed to learn about their natural environment in a manner that harness is the human potential, both spiritually and materially. The stress is on value based learning which gives an opportunity to children to work for each other's well being rather than to permit selfish pursuits.

SSA realizes the value of early childhood care and education and looks upon the 0-14 age as a continuum. It will try to support pre-school learning in ICDS centres or special pre-school centres in non-ICDS areas.

Objectives of Sarva Shiksha Abhiyan

(a) All children in school, Education Guarantee Centre, Alternate School, 'Back to School' camp by 2003.

(b) All children complete five years of primary schooling by 2007.

(c) All children complete eight years of elementary schooling by 2010.

(d) Focus on elementary education of satisfactory quality with emphasis on education for life.

(e) Bridge all gender and social category gaps at primary stage by 2007 and at elementary education level by 2010.

(f) Universal retention by 2010.

The SSA has set up a framework for its implementation. It allows State to formulate context specific guidelines within the overall framework. It encourages district to reflect local specificity. It promotes local need based planning on the lines provided by national policy norms. It aims to make planning a realistic exercise by adopting broad norms.

It is expected that various districts and States are likely to achieve universalization in their own context and time frame. 2010 is the outer limit for achieving the target. The emphasis is on mainstreaming out of school children through diverse strategies so that eight years of schooling for all children in the age group of 6-14 is provided. The thrust is on bridging gender and social gaps and a total retention of all children in schools. It is also expected that the education system will be made more relevant so that children and parents find the schooling system a joyful experience in their own natural and social environment.

The SSA has two important aspects (i) it provides a wide convergent frame work for implementation of elementary education schemes, (ii) it is also a programme with budget allocation for strengthening wider areas to achieve U.E.E. While all investments in the elementary education sector from the States and central plans would reflect as part of SSA framework, they will all merge into the SSA programme within next few years. As a programme it reflects additional resource for U.E.E.

Broad Strategies

1. Institutional reforms : The central and State government will take up reform to improve the efficiency of the delivering system.

2. Sustainable Financing : The SSA is based on the premise that financial intervention has to be sustainable .
3. Community Ownership : The programme calls for community ownership of school based intervention through effective decentralization. This would involve women groups, VEC members and PRIs.
4. Institutional Capacity Building : The SSA conceives a major capacity building for national, State and district level institution such as NIEPA, NCERT, SCERT, SIEMAT, DIET etc.
5. Improvement in quality requires sustainable resource persons.
6. Improving mainstream educational system by infusion of new approaches and adoption of cost effective and efficient methods.
7. Community based monitoring with full transparency.
8. Habitation as a unit of planning.
9. Accountability to the community.
10. Priority to education of girls.
11. Focus on disadvantaged group like SC, ST, minorities and urban deprived children.
12. Thrust on quality - making elementary education useful and relevant for children.
13. The SSA recognizes the central role of teachers and advocates a focus on the development needs through setting up of block/cluster resource centres. Provision of opportunities for teacher development, Focus on class room transaction.
14. District Elementary Education Plan - each district will prepare a plan reflecting all the investment made and required in the elementary education sector with a holistic and convergent approach.

There will be a perspective plan that will give a frame work of activities to achieve U.E.E. There will be also an annual work plan and budget in the whole year.

15. The SSA will commence throughout the country with a well conceived plan which provides a large number of interventions for capacity building. This will include provision for household surveys, community based mapping and training of different personnel, support for setting up infrastructure, diagnostic study etc.

Under SSA provision of elementary education is largely made by government and government aided schools. However, the large number of private unaided school in many part of the country that provide elementary education while encouraging all effort to equity and access to all in well endowed private unaided schools. Efforts will be made to explore areas of public private partnership in this field. In case private sector wishes to develop partnership within the broad parameters of State policy efforts could be made. DIETS and other government teacher training institutions could be used to provide resource support to private unaided institutions, if the additional cost is to be meet by these private bodies.

The assistance under the programme of SSA will be on a 85:15 sharing arrangement between central and State government is the Ninth plan. In the Tenth plan the sharing could be 75:25 and thereafter the cost would be shared equally between the centre and State governments. The State governments will have to maintain level of standard in primary education. The contribution for State share for SSA will over and above this statement. Funds for the mid-day meal so far as the food grains and its transportation cost is concerned would be met by the centre and the cost of cooked meal would be meet by State government.

The SSA has fixed norms for twenty one interventions to be made for the overall upgradation of elementary education :

1. There would be one teacher for every forty children in primary and upper primary schools. There will be atleast two teachers in one school. In the upper primary there should be one teacher for every class.
2. There should be a school or alternative schooling facility within one kilometer of every habitation. Provision has also be made of opening of new schools as per State norms or for setting a Education Guarantee schools in unserved areas.
3. There should be one upper primary school for every two primary schools.
4. Each primary school would have two classrooms with verandah.
5. Free textbooks have to be provided to all girls and SC and ST children at primary and upper primary level within a ceiling of Rs.150 per child.
6. 33% of SSA programme funds would be the ceiling for improvement of school facility and construction of Block Resource Centres/Cluster Resource Centres.
7. Maintenance and repair of school building has to be done by the School Management Committees/ VECs. There is a ceiling of Rs. 5000 per year but it must involve elements of community contribution.
8. There is a provision of Rs. 10.000 per school for Teaching Learning Equipment. In this teachers and parents have to be actively involved.
9. For upper primary schools there is a ceiling of Rs. 50,000 per school. The specific requirement for each school has to be determined by the school committee.
10. Rs. 2,000 per year per primary school has been provided for replacement for non-functional school equipment.

11. The teachers grant has been fixed upto Rs. 5,000 per teacher per year in primary schools.

12. There is provision of 20 days inservice training for all teachers each year, 60 days refresher course for untrained teachers and 30 days orientation for fresh trained recruit. The cost of the training would be Rs. 70 per day.

13. For establishment of State Institute of Educational Management And Training (SIEMAT) each State will be given one time assistance upto Rs. 3 crores. The States have to agree to sustain the institution.

14. In maximum 8 person in a village for two days in a year could be trained as a community leaders. Preference will be given to women in this programme.

15. Upto to twelve hundred rupees has been provided for integration of disabled children per year.

16. Upto to Rs. 1500 per school per year has been provided for research evaluation and monitoring. Priority has to be given for development of capacity for appraisal and supervision. This would include provision for regular school mapping and micro - planning for updating of household data.

17. The management cost should not exceed 6% of the budget of the district plan. This would include expenditure on office expense and hiring of experts at various level. Priority has to be given to experts in M.I.S., Community Planning Process. Civil Works, Gender, etc. Management cost has to be used to develop effective teams at State/District Block/Cluster levels.

18. Provision has also been made upto Rs. 15 lakhs for each innovative project and Rs. 50 lakh for a district per year. The innovative activity will be in the field of girls education, early childhood care and education intervention for SC and ST children

and for Computer education at the upper primary level.

19. Funds have been provided for BRC/CRC buildings. Some funds have been given for purchase of furniture and for contingency.

20. Attention has also been given to intervention for out of school children such as setting up of Education Guarantee Centres at unserved locations, setting up of other alternative models, devising bridge courses, remedial courses and back to school camps with a focus on guiding out of school children into regular schools.

21. As per specific proposal of a district duly recommended by the State, funds have been allocated for preparatory activities. Micro-planning, household surveys, studies, community mobilization, school based activities, office equipment and training and orientation at all levels.

4. Overview :

All the developing countries are addressing the challenge of Education For All since education is most powerful instrument for the alleviation of poverty and inequality in society. This commitment was made in the Jomtein conference in 1990 and was reaffirmed at Dakar in 2000. Great importance has been attached to primary education as it develops the capacity to learn, read and use mathematics and to acquire information and use it for development. Completion of atleast 5-6 years of schooling is a critical threshold for sustainable mastery of basic competencies. The main task is to enroll all children in the official school going age. It is more important to see that they do not drop-out before completion of 5 - 6 years of schooling. This has proved to be a difficult task for many social and economic reasons. It has proven to be a great constraint for girls, SC, ST and the poor in India.

There has been a phenomenonal growth of primary education schools from 1950-51 to 2001-02. The growth is seen in enrolment of both boys and girls. The gender gap has also narrowed down to a large extent. The same is true of Scheduled castes and tribes. The gap between the drop-out rate of boys and girls has also gone down. However, the public expenditure in India on primary education is much below of many of the south asian countries. It is necessary to raise this considering the educational backwardness of the country.

In recent decades a number of initiatives and interventions have been made by the State and the NGOs in the field of primary education. The most wide spread initiative was in the form of District Primary Education Programme (DPEP) which aimed at provision of access to all children to primary education, reduction in drop-out rates and reducing the gap among gender and weaker sections and to decentralize learning and implementation of administration of primary education. This task was taken up in a number of States. 85% of the funding being provided by the Central Government . This effort was made possible by soft loans by UNICEF, European Union and organization like ODA (U.K.), SIDA, etc. Under this initiative the Bihar Education Project was started in 1991. Besides bringing about qualitative and quantitative improvement in selected districts its Mahila Samakhya component has done remarkable work in the empowerment of women. It has made women conscious of their right, and raise the level of their assertiveness and self confidence. The Shiksha Karmi and Lok Jumbish programme has made a profound impression on the primary education scenario in Rajasthan. Decentralized and participatory functioning and intregation with the main education system are the chief feature of this project. The interventions made by the government in the field of primary education in Himachal Pradesh has shown that political will and the willing cooperation of administration and society can produce miracles. From an educationally backward State in early 1960s has been catapulated to the second position in the field of literacy and primary education in country at the turn of last century.

The most important intervention at the national level is the Sarva Shiksha Abhiyan. It seeks to achieve the goal of universalization of primary education by 2010. Children in all States would completed five years of schooling or its equivalent through non-formal means by the year 2005. The unique feature of SSA is that it is aimed at community ownership of the entire school system at the primary level. The emphasis is not only on the quantitative spread of education to bring all children in the age group of 6- 11 in the educational net but also to improve it qualitatively. In fact all primary education activities have been taken over under the SSA umbrella.

References

Anuradha De, Claire Naroha & Meera Samson (2002): Primary Education in Himachal Pradesh : Examing A Success Story, in, Govinda, R., Indian Education Report, Oxford University Press, New Delhi.

Department of Education (2004) : Selected Educational Statistics, Ministry of H.R.D., Govt. of India, New Delhi.

Department of Education (2004) : Sarva Shiksha Abhiyan, Ministry of H.R.D., Govt. of India, New Delhi.

Govinda, R (ed) (2004): India Education Report, Oxford University Press, New Delhi.

Jandhyala, B. G. Tilak (2002) : Financing Elementary Education in India, in, Govinda, R., (ed), Indian Education Report, Oxford University Press, New Delhi.

Ministry of Human Resource Development and National Institute of Educational Planning and Administration (2000) : Education For All : India, New Delhi.

Probe (1999) : Public Report On Basic Education In India, Oxford University Press, New Delhi.

Sumitra Chowdhury (2002) : Universal Elementary Education In Rajasthan : A Study with Focus on Innovative Strategies, in Govinda, R. (ed), Indian Education Report, Oxford University Press, New Delhi.

2

ROLE OF FAMILY, COMMUNITY AND SCHOOL FACTORS IN IMPROVING RETENTION AND THE ACHIEVEMENT LEVEL OF DISADVANTAGED CHILDREN

Niraj Kumar

Background

At the time of independence in 1947, India inherited an education system which covered a small population and was characterized by striking regional and structural disparities. Only 16% of the population was literate and one child out of three had been enrolled in primary school. The low level of literacy and enrolment were compounded by acute regional and gender disparities. Recognizing that education is vitally linked with the totality of the development process, the reform and restructuring of the educational system was accepted as an important area of State intervention. Accordingly the need for a literate population and universal education for all children in the 6 - 14 age group was provided with a precisely defined and delineated frame work in the Indian Constitution as well as in successive Five year plans.

Even though Indian official policy is education for all, there is a glaring disparity in the achievement among the different sections of the population. The literacy rates of SC and ST are very low and they are still lower in case of their women folk. The enrolment rate in Class I to V, VI to VIII and IX to XI reveals an extremely low level of education of the literate population as a whole. The national policy of prescribing a uniform curriculum and emphasizing competitive achievement has failed to provide a universal school system in India.

Now after five decades of our independence, there is no discrimination in admission to educational institutions but socio-economic factors compel several segments of the population remaining socially and educationally backward. Generally groups vulnerable to social discrimination also suffer from economic deprivation. It was estimated in the early eighties that 37% of the population in the country is below the poverty line with almost 40 million working children in different regions. The participation of girls, scheduled castes, scheduled tribes and physically handicapped still remains a challenge despite many improvement in access at primary level.

The failure of SCs, STs and women to get some kind of education is reason enough to conclude that throughout the last five decades the government has reneged on its Constitutional commitment to draw these sections into its mainstream by its failure to effectively implement the special Constitutional provisions for their social and educational advancement. Naturally this has become embarrassing for India in its new era of economic internationalism as it seeks to participation in global economy.

Amongst the deprived sections of the population, women are doubly disadvantaged, suffering from an unequal status in the family as well as in society. Facilities for education are equally available for both boys and girls, yet their is significantly lower level of utilization of facilities by girls and women. The drop-out rates of girls at the primary as well as the upper primary level are higher than those of boys. The literacy rate of women is at the same level as that of men three decade ago. There are besides, wide regional variations in female literacy ranging from near universal literacy in Kerala to a paltry 21% in Rajasthan. Gender disparity and regional imbalance at both the State and the urban-rural levels are thus among the major factor that continue to operate in the sphere of education.

The gap between boys and girls participation in elementary education is the biggest single gap that needs to be filled for Universalization of Elementary Education. The problem of UEE is, in essence, the problem of the girl child. The gender disparity, particularly in the rural areas, reflects the discriminatory social attitudes to the girl child. While the solution of this problem does not lie entirely in the educational system, education can and should play a positive interventionist role in the improvement of women's status. Both demand and supply side interventions are called for to be attitudinal as well as monetary. The main demand side interventions have been :

(a) Programme for awareness generation among women, amongst which the most successful and reputed is the Mahila Samakhya, a women's empowerment project which does not aim at service delivery but seeks to bring about a change in women's perception about themselves and that of society in regard to women's traditional roles.

(b) Incentive schemes which reduce the direct costs of Education Incentive Schemes of different kinds are already a well established feature of elementary school system. These are almost wholly funded by the States. The coverage and extent vary widely. In all States education is free upto Class XII for girls. Many States also provides incentives by way of uniforms, free textbooks and attendance.

(c) Linkages between schools with ECCE centres and creches.

The main supply side interventions have been :

(a) Gender sensitization of the education system and its functionaries so that gender concern is reflected across the board in all educational programmes, more particularly in the area of basic education.

(b) Recruitment of more female teachers. The proportion of female teachers have been increasing gradually in 1990, 31.61% of the primary school teachers were women compared to 15% in 1950 - 51. There is however, a concentration of women teachers in urban areas and inter-State disparities are conspicuous. In 1998 in Uttar Pradesh, there was 25.49% women teachers in comparison to 67.66% in Kerala.

(c) Effective NFE programmes.

(d) The central focus in the SC's educational development is their equalization, in all areas and in all four dimensions - rural female, urban female, rural male and urban male.

The measure contemplated for this purpose include :

(a) Incentives to indigent families to send their children to school regularly till they reach the age of 14.

(b) Scholarship from Class I onwards for children of families engaged in occupations such as scavenging, flaying and tanning. All children of such families, regardless of income levels will be covered by this scheme and time bounded programmes targeted on them will be undertaken.

(c) Constant micro-planning and verification to ensure that the enrolment, retention and successful completion of courses by SC students do not fall at any stage and provision for remedial courses to improve their prospects for further education and employment.

(d) Recruitment of teachers from Scheduled castes which as a matter of fact was 11.84% in 1998 in Uttar Pradesh.

(e) Provision of facilities for SC students hostel at district headquarters, according to a phased programmes.

(f) Location of school building in such a way as to facilitate full participation of the Scheduled castes.

(g) Constant innovation in finding new methods to increase the participation of the Scheduled castes in the educational process.

(h) The following measures were taken to bring the Scheduled tribes on par with others:

(i) The socio-culture milieu of the STs has its distinctive characteristics including, in many cases, their own spoken language. This underlines the need to develop the curricula and device instructional materials in tribal language at the initial stage, with arrangements for switching over to the regional language.

(ii) Educated and promising Scheduled tribes youth's will be encouraged and trained to take up teaching in tribal areas as they are still lagging behind and their proportion was 7.65% on the National level and in the State of Uttar Pradesh only 0.40% in the year 1998.

(iii) Residential schools, including Ashram schools will be established on a large scale as their effectiveness has been demonstrated in many States.

(iv) Incentive schemes are being formulated for the Scheduled tribes keeping in view their special needs and life styles, special remedial courses and other programmes to remove psycho-social impediments will be provided to improve their performance in various courses.

(v) The curriculum is being designed to create an awareness of the rich culture heritage of the tribal people as also of their enormous creative talent.

(vi) Plan of action, 1992 seeks to achieve universal enrolment of disabled children in general school, in special schools, and in special sections of general schools for children who required such special education. It also envisages reduction of drop-out rates among disabled children to bring them on par with general drop-out rates by adjustment and adaptation of curriculum and teaching to the special needs of the children and reorienting pre-service and in-service teachers training programme.

The story of inequality in Indian education continues. The picture worsens when one looks at the situation regarding the education of minorities. Articles 29 and 30 of the Constitution of India guarantee the rights of minorities to conserve their language, script and culture and to establish and administer educational institutions of their choice whether based on religion or language. However the implementation of the above has at best been uneven. For example Muslims make up 11.4% of the Indian population and yet it is estimated that as little as 20% of Muslim population complete more than five years of schooling.

Contemporary situation of disadvantaged children

While the Gross Enrolment Ratio (GER) at the primary stage in the country as a whole and in most of its States exceed 100% there are quite a few States where the ratio is considerably lower. Girls enrolment at the primary stage has grown appreciably from 6 million in 1950-51 to 43 million in 1991-92. The growth rate of girls enrolment has been higher than that of boys but disparities still remain. In Uttar Pradesh according to the Sixth All India Education Survey (1998) the GER for the State was 63.27% out of which 50.63% was for girls in comparison of 74.59% for boys.

Scheduled castes and Scheduled tribes constitute the officially recognized weaker sections of society and form a distinct target group under the existing pattern of planning. The affirmative policies of the Government has resulted in a considerable increase in the enrolment of SC's and ST's at the primary stage.

However, wide regional variations are to be found in both SC and ST group. SC girls in the State of Kerala, for instance are likely to be better informed than non-SC boys in some of the more backward States and districts. The participation of SC's and ST's at the primary level is now more or less in proportion to their percentage share in the population. As in the other groups, drop-outs amongst SCs and STs declined over the years but are still significantly large with marked gender disparities in participation. In the year 1998 in the State of Uttar Pradesh, the population of SC consisted 21.05% of the total population and their enrolment rate was 26.81%. Likewise the enrolment rate of ST was 0.37% and their composition in the population was 0.21%. This shows some positive inclinations but universal participation is still far off.

Research available on the education of women in India points to a multiplicity of socio-cultural and economic factors that stand at the root of India's male dominated society. The prevailing cultural norms of gender behaviour and the perceived domestic and reproductive roles of women tend to adversely affect the education of girls. Negative attitudes to girls schooling, maintaining them in school for five years, to their mobility, especially after puberty, all reflect dominant male values and attitudes that keep girl's and women in their place.

The female disadvantage in basic education links with some deep rooted features of gender relations in

Uttar Pradesh. The gender division of labour, which relegates most adult women including those with relatively good education to domestic work, diminish the perceived returns of investment in female education. The prevailing norms of village exogamy and patrilocal post martial residence imply that these returns and other benefits of female education flow primarily to a daughter's future in-laws rather than to her parents. The remarkably backward state of female education in Uttar Pradesh fits in a tight web of mutually reinforcing gender inequalities and patriarchal practices.

Caste continues to be an important determinant of educational achievements and school attendance independently of income and parental education. But it is hard to ascertain, for instance, to what extent the schooling system causes discrimination which is quite widespread and includes : (i) discrimination against Scheduled caste settlements in the location of schools. (ii) teachers refusing to touch Scheduled caste children, (iii) children from particular castes being special target of verbal abuse and physical punishment by the teachers, (iv) low - caste children being frequently beaten by higher caste classmates.

While the gap in educational aspirations between different social groups is narrowing rapidly, these common aspirations give very unequal attention to boys and girls. Most parents (mother no less than fathers) express much stronger interest in their son's education than in their daughters.

Apart from the social and economic constraints in the context of EFA, it is not only to ensure that children attend school. The quality of education is also of paramount concern. New knowledge, skills and values transmitted are as important as what is learned. Most of the students who are targeted under EFA programme are first generation learners. Neither themselves nor their guardians are keen to attain education. At this juncture, the role of teachers and the school atmosphere becomes important. The DPEP interventions are ensuring education to a very large number of first generation learners, some of whom may face considerable barriers in the school environment. Thus strong affirmative action is required to retain first generation learners, especially in the first two years of schooling. This is true particularly for girls. This requires teachers to have a special set of practical skills to deal with the disadvantaged children within the classroom.

Now the schools are emerging as a hub for targeted planning and implementation. It is evident that the school based plans are beginning to produce results with the participation of village communities and school education committees. However, in many instances, school plans are merely concerned with utilization of school grants or infrastructure improvements. There appears to be obvious and enthusiastic participation of communities, headmasters and teachers in micro planning and school mapping exercises. However, they do not yet seem to be translated into activities and would reflect specific development goals for the schools improvement.

The current scenario of primary education clearly reveals that universalizing primary education by 2005 A.D. is very difficult and needs tremendous efforts to achieve the desired goal. The government at the centre needs to mobilize all agencies to rejuvenate the educational system for the benefit of the masses. There cannot be two opinions that Indian economic and social development should include areas of health, cultural values and welfare.

The seven point guideline, worked out by the Government in consultation with the States / Union Territories to achieve the objective of universalization of primary education is as follows :

1. Finding the problems of school dropouts and identifying suitable measures on retention and achievement rather than an enrolment.

2. Identifying educationally backward districts rather than the States to implement the programmes of universalization of education.
3. Providing universal access to education facilities to girls, socially backward groups, school dropout and working labour.
4. Implementing various universaliation programmes for up-gradation of classroom, environment, competence of teachers, their training and motivation.
5. Participative approach should be practiced more in the process of mobilization and motivation in the overall planning and management of universalization of primary education.
6. Converting different schemes of universalization of primary education and related services such as early childhood.
7. Implementation of non-formal education system for working children, rural girls, socially backward and marginalized section of the society.

The need of the hour is that these points be implemented with a certain degree of flexibility that would go a long way in helping to achieve the objective of universalization of primary education. These initiatives also taken together, represents the new concept of education, shaped by the convention of the rights of the child, the world summit for children and the world declaration on education for all.

State And District Profile

Uttar Pradesh according to the Sixth All India Educational Survey has 63 districts comprising of 901 blocks and 112803 inhabited villages. There are 60.5% primary schools within habitation, 12.65% schools upto

0.5 km. and 2.87% schools are situated at more than 2 km. The State has 86539 primary schools, out of which 55.22% has drinking water facility, 25.27% has urinal, 11.17% has separate urinal for girls, 17.38% has lavatory for girls.

The overall literacy rate of the State is 57.36%. For male it is 70.23% and for female it is 42.98%. The State showed a decadal growth of 16.65% in the area of literacy (2001). Indian Human Development Report, NCEAR, 1999, reveals that the dropout rate in the age group of 6 - 14 years in U. P. for the household whose yearly income is upto Rs. 20,000/- is 4.4% where as in the income group of above Rs. 62,000/- it is 3.2%. Muslims have a higher dropout rate of 7% followed by 4.3% among SC / ST and 3.8% in the general population. In the 6-14 years of age group about 56.3% student dropout in government aided schools and 27.2% in private schools.

According to the UNFPA report, India : Towards Population And Development Goals, 1997, the combined enrolment ratio of 6-10 years students at primary level in Uttar Pradesh is 61.1%. In the rural areas it is 58.8% and 72.1% in urban areas. On the issue of enrolment in Class V as of Class I enrolment, in other words known as "survival" was 43.0% in 1978. It increased to 58.6% in 1998 but again slipped to 47.4% in the year 1993. Thus the average annual change between the years 1978-86 was 4.5% and between 1986-93 it was 2.7%. This shows that between 1986-93 the overall impact of efforts made by the schools, administration and community was poor.

In Basti district there are 13 blocks and the overall literacy rate of the district is 59.7%. Basti Sadar block which is situated about half kilometer from the district has the highest literacy rate (64%) has a total of 133 primary schools out of which 14 are private (unaided). Altogether there are 366 teachers excluding 8 Siksha Mitra. Number of Nyay Panchayati Resource Center

(NPRC) is 10 and 80 VEC are constituted in the whole block. Students belonging to SC category are much larger in number in comparison to other categories in the total of 14314 students.

Kudraha is another block of the district where the literacy rate is 42%, lowest in the district. Altogether there are 143 teachers excluding 35 Siksha Mitra in the block. Total number of schools is 111, out of which 8 are private unaided schools. NPRC is 9 in number and there are 60 VEC. In this block OBC students are in larger number.

The overall literacy rate of Sidharthnagar district is 43.97%. It has a total of 13 blocks. Barhani block which is situated at a distance of 41 km from the district headquarter has a lowest literacy rate in the district. Altogether there are 100 primary schools, out of which 15 are private unaided schools. Total number of teachers are 82 for teaching 7152 students in the block.

In Dumariaganj block which is situated at a distance of 52 km from the district headquarter, the total number of schools are 200. The literacy rate is 40.4%, maximum in any block of the district. Altogether there are 179 teachers for 18,862 students. Number of NPRC is 16 and VEC is 114.

Present Study

For the purpose of achieving universalisation of Elementary Education (UEE) the District Primary Education Programme (DPEP) was conceived as a centrally sponsored programme with the approval of the Central Advisory Board of Education (CABE). DPEP is a home grown idea that focuses on contextuality which takes care of the diversities that exist in the vast country like ours. But the flip side to the achievement of DPEP programme and the literacy campaign is that out of 200 million children in the age group of 6 to 14 years, 59 million children are yet not attending school. Of this,

35 millions are girls and 24 millions are boys. There are also at least one lakh habitations in the country without schooling facilities within one kilometer.

The situation in Uttar Pradesh is not different from the national scenario. Still the increase in retention and achievement level have not been uniformly attained by the girls, SC/ST and other disadvantaged groups students. Thus the present study aims to describe accurately the ground level realities and the stake of different agencies in uplifting the retention and achievement level of students belonging to disadvantaged category. Thus the study included five objectives, viz. : (i) Role of community including VEC in increasing, enrolment, retention and achievement level of the disadvantaged children, (ii) Interface between community, parents and teachers, (iii) Role of family economy and personal education of family members in planning the education of their children, (iv) Role of teachers, school infrastructure and atmosphere and the impact of different government sponsored provisions in retaining the students, and (v) To identify loopholes which are constraints in increasing the enrolment and retention of children.

Methodology

Eastern Uttar Pradesh is the universe for the study. The samples were drawn on the basis of multistage sampling. Two districts, Basti and Sidharthnagar which are under DPEP II were chosen for the study. Basti Sadar and Kudraha blocks for Basti and Barhani and Dumariaganj blocks for Sidharthnagar were selected for detailed study. In both the districts the total number of sample was 1930 out of which 900 were parents, 77 teachers, 160 VEC members and 790 students. Data regarding the study have been collected through interview schedules, interview guides, observation notes and group discussions.

Findings

Table 1 : Response of VEC members on educational issues

Issues	Response (Yes)
Children in school going age are enrolled	61.25%
Girls go to school	59.62%
Efforts made to send children school who are not enrolled	85.62%
Classes are conducted on time	93.75%
Tried to increase the achievement level of students	70.00%
Increase in enrolment due to more government assistance	97.50%
Regular meetings of VEC	65.00%
Women and persons from deprived community take part in meetings	52.50%

It was observed during the study that respondents admitted the importance of their children education, but only in case of female children people had different local excuse. VEC members claimed that classes were conducted on time, but what they said was mainly based on hearsay. Some members even hesitated to pass any negative remark on the existing educational situation because they felt that they have no right to do so in view of their limited participation in ongoing educational activities.

Even if it is assumed that the VEC meetings are taking place regularly the participation of members is poor. Some VEC members told us that meetings take place regularly but failed to elaborate the agenda and outcome of previous meetings.

Despite so much emphasis by the government on the importance of the role of VEC at the village level, more efforts are needed to make it fully functional. What the committee members and school administration has learnt so far is to maintain the up-to-date meeting register of the proceedings. They do not worry about its implementation. Members are happy to claim respect from the school administration. Many of the VEC members have no idea about their role, authority and responsibility.

On the other hand the local school teachers are afraid of the VEC members. Teachers are aware of the authority vested in the VEC by the government and therefore they always remain vigilant towards their duty. Similarly the interaction between the teachers and the VEC members regarding the overall development of education is increasing. VEC members are now more punctual than before in utilization of government funds and in distribution of government incentives among the children of disadvantaged communities. VEC is also now under pressure to show better results for the overall betterment of education and many of them have produced good results.

Table 2 : Reasons for poor enrolment of children belonging to disadvantaged group according to VEC members

Reasons	Frequency
Guardian's reluctance	63.12%
Poor economic condition	50.00%
Involve as child labour	48.75%
Deteriorating standard of education	3.75%
Deteriorating conditions of the school	0.62%

It is evident that most of the VEC members feel that guardian 's reluctance was the main reason for children in this group to fail to get atleast the initial five years of primary schooling. Poor economic condition of the family also keep the child out of school. Guardian's reluctance and poor economic condition of the family ultimately forces the child to share domestic chores and even out side. Thus the child is deprived of education and sometimes the enrolled child becomes a drop-out.

The plight of full time child labour is indeed distressing. Even for part time child workers engaged in family labour, work is not always compatible with schooling. At times of peak agricultural activity, for instance, poor family may be under great pressure to engage children as full time labour.

Some VEC members told that some section of disadvantaged group are totally indifferent to their children's education. Their reservation is based on their experience of educated youths in their community who failed to achieve anything. Education as a means for personality development and a tool for interacting in every day life has no meaning for them.

Table 3 : Response of parents on educational issues

Issues	**Response (Yes)**
Quality of education	85.22%
Education of girl children	99.66%
Good relationship between parents and teachers	63.22%
Go to school to meet teachers	15.66%
Aware of VEC activities	23.66%
Satisfaction over the performance of the school	33.55%
Adequate school infrastructure	46.55%

Majority of parents were of the view that their children are getting quality education although they do not have any parameter to judge what quality means. Similarly on the issue of girls education, bulk of respondents did not feel uncomfortable when they replied about discrimination against girls.

Teacher - parent interaction has been a part of UEE agenda. Field experience and the data collected reveal that in reality some teachers fail to move in this direction as a part of their duty to accelerate the pace of DPEP. They have many excuse, as the parents do not turn up when invited or in case of disadvantaged group the parents fail to utilize the opportunity of these meetings. In reality both the sides are committing mistake. But considering the importance of this issue and the objective of UEE, the teachers are expected to encourage the parents on their part. In some places the ego of teachers based on caste prejudices becomes evident on this issue. They require a change in their mind set.

There are few studies that have actually explored teacher attitudes to Dalit children though the fact of social discrimination in classroom processes suggests that teachers tend to reproduce discriminatory attitudes and practices that underlie caste relations in society. Anitha's study in Karnataka reports that Dalit pupils were called 'Kadu-jana' (forest people) who would not learn without beating (2000). The message that teachers appear to be giving to children is the inherently poor scholastic abilities of Dalit children, the lack of interest of parents, and the inevitability of their class (caste) status. Similarly Jabbi and Rajyalakshmi's interviews with women and children from Dalit / tribal communities in their study in Bihar brought forth complaints about 'teachers' irregularity, absenteeism, negligence and utilizing services of the children for their personal work, poor quality of teaching and so on. Nambissan (2001) also in a study of Rajasthan noted that 'fear of teachers as well as corporal punishment' are factors that parents (mainly of SC children) cite as constraining regular attendance. But on the other hand Anitha (2000) also suggests that teachers who are sensitive to the difficult circumstances that Dalit children come from and who respond to their educational needs with a positive attitude do facilitate the education of such children.

Table 4 : Reasons of low enrolment and discontinuation according to parents

Response	Frequency
Poverty	45.44%
Domestic work	44.66%
Guardian's apathy	31.66%
Religious factors	0.55%
Lack of government resource	0.55%
Lack of interest among children	4.11%

Most of the parents hold the view that poverty is the basic reason for which children leave education. This was followed by the view that the demand for domestic work also forces the children to abstain from school, especially the girls. These both factors compel the guardians and they become less enthusiastic towards their children education as is evident from the above data. Very few parents attributed religious constraints for poor enrolment in government primary schools.

Economic hardships of the parents has a bearing on their planning for children education. DPEP has to a great extent offset this issue by providing many incentives to the children of disadvantaged communities in cash and kind. Free textbooks, stationary and in some areas school uniform other than scholarship and midday meal has provided some relief to the parents. Naturally this has reduced the parent's excuse of keeping their children out of school.

The role of public policy in providing incentives for education (textbooks, midday meals, etc) and thereby reducing the direct costs of schooling has been seen as crucial in addressing educational deprivation. The midday meal programme in particular has been seen to encourage school enrolment and attendance and to raise the nutritional status of children as well. The PROBE report (1999) notes that 'in areas where school meals are operational, most teachers take the view that they have boosted school attendance, and parents share this view.

But at the same time a large section of the families in the disadvantaged category are below the poverty line and agriculture and other wage labour is their primary occupation, especially in rural areas. Poverty is likely to continue to be a major deterrent to education despite growing aspiration for education among these people, which has been documented in a number of recent studies. N.S.S.O. data (1993-94) do show that proportion of children who do not attend school sharply increases in lower monthly per capita expenditure groups.

Srivastava's recent study (1999) of living conditions in villages of Uttar Pradesh and Bihar indicates that while almost half of the total SC children are out of school, 60% of the poorest SC children are not in school but in Bihar, two -third of the poorest SC children are not in school.

Among the poor, the extent to which households experience some security of livelihood is also likely to determine whether children are sent to school, how regularly they attend school and how long they are able to continue their education. Irregular income, frequent migration in search of work, or the death or illness of a breadwinner is likely to make children from these households dropouts.

Table 5 : Reasons for school visit by the parents

Response	Frequency
Occasionally	42.88%
Visit without invitation	38.44%
On special occasions	9.55%
When called by authorities	8.22%
Any other	0.88%

Parent - teacher meetings in a formal way was totally absent. Schools are generally within the village and therefore on one pretext or the other the parents make a casual visit to the school. These visits can not be considered as visit to discuss the performance of their children in the school. Caste also plays a vital role in parent - teacher meet. Generally teachers from upper caste do not like meeting parents of lower caste. Similarly teachers from lower caste are shy of meeting higher caste parents.

Decentralization of education and local level participation of Dalits and other marginalized groups are increasingly being stressed in policy documents. Village level committees that are being constituted are statutorily required to comprise a minimum number of members from the 'weaker sections'. However, caste relations that predominate at the village level make the notion of 'community' itself problematic and this needs to be addressed. Commenting on village - level committees in her study in Karnataka, Kaul (2001) notes that "participation of Dalits was not easily acceptable to the dominant castes. Sometimes the representation of SC group was only on paper. The School Betterment Committee in urban areas also included Dalit representatives, but very few such members attended committee meetings because they felt they would not be in a position to make any difference to the school functioning".

Table 6 : Reasons for girl's education given by teachers

Issues	Response (Yes)
Feeling of equality	55.84%
To participate in social development	53.24%
To be self dependent	44.15%
To be helpful in family well being	36.36%
Any other	2.59%

The response to education of girls involves a number of socio-cultural and economic factors which form the basis of our male dominated society. Negative attitude towards girls schooling and restricting their mobility especially after puberty hampers their educational aspirations.

Pande (2001) in her study of Uttar Pradesh notes that among the disadvantaged sections, a girl child is more likely to attend young siblings and take care of old people than a male child. Thus the relatively large dropout of girls belonging to disadvantaged section of the society needs serious attention. However studies show that the presence of educated members within poor household, especially mothers who are literate and have some schooling, does increase the participation of children, particularly girls, in school (Vaidyanathan and Nair, 2001).

Educational disparities between disadvantaged castes have not received adequate attention. Some castes have been able to avail of opportunities for education and new occupations, and thereby, better their social conditions relative to other castes. Thus Pai (2001) speaks of 'new inequalities' that have been created by the present policies of affirmative action and the social conflict that results as the competition between castes for scarce resource heightens.

Increased focus on educational achievement in India began around 1980 with the preparation of document called "Minimum Level of Learning' (MLL) by the National Council of Educational Research and Training (NCERT) as a framework for preparing local - specific learning packages. Following this, a battery of criterion referenced achievement tests were prepared to measure learning achievements of pupils in Language and Mathematics for Classes I to IV. A large level national survey of learning levels was also conducted.

The idea of MLL was reiterated by an Experts Committee appointed by the Government of India in 1991. The MLL, as a strategy for improving quality of elementary education was incorporated in policy documents as an attempt to combine equity with quality. It laid down learning outcomes in the form of compentencies or level of learning for each stage and grade of elementary education. The strategy also outlined the adoption of measures that would ensure achievement of these level of children in both formal and non-formal education (NFE) centres. Almost all major States have now adopted the MLL, translated these into regional languages and developed textbooks, teachers guide and teacher training materials.

Table 7: Achievement level test of disadvantaged students of Class V

Achievement Level	Boys		Girls	
	Language	Math	Language	Math
0%	—	—	—	—
1 to 40%	60.35%	62.37%	70.04%	90.17%
41 to 60%	31.81%	34.84%	21.91%	9.31%
61 to 80%	7.82%	2.77%	5.03%	0.50%
Above 80%	—	—	—	—

Performance-wise the achievement level of boys are comparatively better than girls in both the subjects. Although non of the students in any category advanced his or her achievement level to Mastery level but at the same time gradual impact of DPEP in the State to increase an average achievement by 25% seems to be emerged. Thus achievement figures when examined against the reasonably high standards set by MLL, suggest that the quality of learning remains a matter of concern in government supported schools across the country which otherwise for a long remained neglected.

Overview

Children from the disadvantaged communities have lagged behind in education for a long time. The participation of girls, SC and ST children is lower in comparison to other sections of society. The National Policy of Education (1986) and the Programme of Action (1992) provided enabling environment and opened opportunities for reform in primary education sector through DPEP.

Still some of the parents are biased against girls education. Mostly in north Indian families, parents tend to think of a daughter's upbringing mainly from the point of view of her marriage. These social norms, of course, are changing overtime, but they still have a strong hold today in rural areas. Certainly such a mindset is a major constraint in the education of girls among the disadvantaged communities.

The disadvantage of the girls in basic education links with some deep rooted features of gender relations. The gender division of labour, which relegates most adult women including those with relatively good education to domestic work, diminished the perceived norms of village exogamy and patrilocal post - marital residence imply that these returns and other benefits of female education flow primarily to a daughter's future in laws rather than to her parents.

On the part of parents they find justification for keeping their children out of school in many of the long established traditions and system of living. A major justification is economic. Children have traditionally participated in work at even a tender age. They are regarded as a reserve pool of cheap manpower. The vacation also do not synchronize with the agriculture season. The engagement of girls in domestic works may be one of the reasons why the figures of their enrolment and attendance at school are lower than those of boys. The duration of girl's education is shorter as they have to become housewives for whom schooling was not required. Even if they entered primary schools, after few years of schooling, custom and the need to keep girls at home keep them from continuing in school.

Thus poverty continues to be a major impediment in the education of these children and costs of education, as well as children's contribution to work, remains serious issues to be continued. The present policy of providing incentives to children is unlikely to address the constraint of poverty in relation to education. Where children's work is concerned, the larger issue to be addressed is that of sustainable livelihoods of the poor. On the other hand if school reach out to these communities with meaningful education that is attractive to young children, allow for flexibility in timings and schedules for children who work, and provide academic support that they invariably need, it is likely that very young children can be prevented from becoming workers by default, and the entry of older children into the workforce can be delayed.

Quality of education is an important issue and one that needs to be seriously addressed in the larger context of what is seen as the breakdown of the government system of "free education" and the increasing privatization of education even at primary stage. Further, the shift of official policy towards alternate and innovative schools for educationally deprived communities merits serious attention. In the larger context of equity, and education without discrimination as a fundamental right of the child, it would be important to ensure that "alternate" and 'innovative' schools do not become inferior systems of schooling for those who have hitherto been educationally deprived.

The achievement level of the students from the disadvantaged section is still poor. They do not appear to have the proper knowledge of their class text books. In many districts teachers do not fail students at primary level in any class as part of official practice. Thus this practice militates again the objective of DPEP to raise achievement level of students. Teachers at the same time have not devised any mechanism to meet this situation.

Despite DPEP effort, the teacher - student ratio in schools are not upto the mark. Still there are many schools with only one teacher and that also Siksha Mitra. This creates a problem for the students while the teacher is away for attaining meeting at BRC or when he goes for training. Despite this problem, teachers reported that they give extra attention on teaching of medically and physically handicapped students.

The role of teachers and school atmosphere is very crucial as many of the students in school from the disadvantaged communities are first generation learners. Some of them face psychological problems in school environment, especially the girls. For this the teachers are required to have a set of practical skills to deal with the disadvantaged children within the classroom. A beginning needs to be made through sensitization of teachers to caste discrimination during training programmes, squarely addressing the issue of caste relations and human rights in curricula, evolving enabling pedagogies, and providing specific academic support to disadvantaged children. In addition schools need to reach out to them and strengthen school-community relations.

Thus at the end of the 1990s, the gap between the constitutional commitment of education for all children upto the age of 14 years and the actual participation of disadvantaged children in schools remains large and is likely to continue. The role of effective State policy and political will is critical if education of all children including disadvantaged children is to be ensured, particularly in the context of the demand being made of the education in the last few decades. The changing knowledge and skills package that will increasingly determine the future life chances requires that EFA must mean more than basic, and indeed, school education. Education is thus of importance not only because of its critical linkages with human capabilities and empowerment, but also because in industrial terms, in the globalizing world of today, lack of education will widen disparities between and within societies. The education of disadvantaged communities children in India must continue to be a serious concern.

References

Anitha, B.K. (2000) : Village Caste And Education, Rawat Publication, New Delhi.

Govinda, R. (2002) : India Education Report, Oxford University Press, New Delhi.

Jabbi, M. and C. Rajyalakshmi (2001) : Education of Marginalised Social Groups In Bihar, in Vaidyanathan, A. and P. R. Gopinathan Nair (eds), Elementary Education in Rural India : A Grassroots View, Sage Publications, New Delhi.

Kumar, N. (2002) : A Diagnostic Study of Khagaria District Under Sarva Shiksha Abhiyan, Sulabh Institute of Development Studies, Patna.

Kumar, N. (et al) (2002) : A Study of Role of Family, Community and School Factors in Improving Retention And The Achievement Level of Disadvantaged Children, Sulabh Institute of Development Studies, Patna.

Nambissan, Geetha B. (2001) : Social Diversity and Regional disparities in Schooling : A Study of Rural Rajasthan, in Vaidyanathan, A and P. R. Gopinathan Nair (eds), Elementary Education in Rural India : A Grassroot View, Sage Publications, New Delhi.

National Sample Survey Organization (1997) : Economic Activities and School Attendance by Children of India, Report No. 412, Department of Statistics, Govt. of India, New Delhi.

N.C.E.R.T. (1998) : Sixth All India Educational Survey, New Delhi.

Pai, Sudha (2000) : Changing Socio-Economic and Political Profile of Scheduled Castes in Uttar Pradesh, Journal of Indian School of Political Economy, Vol. - 12, Number 3 and 4.

Pande, Anuradha (2001) : Education of Rural Children in U. P. Himalayas, in Vaidyanathan, A. and P. R. Gopinathan Nair (eds), Elementary Education in Rural India : A Grassroot View, Sage Publications, New Delhi.

Probe (1999) : Public Report on Basic Education in India, Oxford University Press, New Delhi.

Srivastava, R. (1999) : Inequality and Education Security, Indian Journal of Labour Economics, Vol. 42, No. 3.

UNFPA (1997) : Towards Population And development Goals, Oxford University Press, New Delhi.

Vaidyanathan, A. and P. R. Gopinathan Nair (Eds) (2001) : Elementary Education in Rural India : A Grassroot View, Sage Publications, New Delhi.

3

PRIVATE SCHOOLS AND UNIVERSAL ELEMENTARY EDUCATION

Niraj Kumar

From the close of the last century there is a growing disenchantment with the State's involvement in many fields, ranging from manufacturing steel and generating electricity to running schools and hospitals. Government is seen as a high cost provider of low quality goods and services, smothered by its own mammoth size, its rules and regulations and its proneness to corruption. Tardy progress in the field of literacy and primary education is seen as yet another example of this. It is not surprising that the call for greater involvement of the private sector and for reduced role of the government in providing goods and services is seen to apply to schooling as well.

Private schools have a right to exist under the Constitution, irrespective of whether they are recognized and aided by the State. In fact, diversity in educational pattern has always been accepted and acknowledged in the country. Educational efforts of individuals of vision, of community groups, of leaders of various social reform movements as well as of the government have worked in tandem, communities have operated schools along side government schools, sometimes to offer education with particular ethnic, religious, political, or other orientation. Thus a pluralistic framework of education and a variety of delivery mechanisms within this have been in place for a long while. However, private educational initiatives have gained new prominence in recent years, though in a somewhat different way from the old as substitutes for, not supplements to, government schools. There is now a popular perception that increased parental demand for education on the one hand and the declining quality of government schools on the other hand will inevitably lead to greater reliance on the private sector.

In case of private schooling, in colonial times, the school system of the metropolitan country was emulated, in diluted form in India. It has been changed only slightly after independence . Like all institutional structures, the system embodies strong vested interests of those who serve the schools and are served by them, it even tends to set the pattern within which the ambitions of a reformer are moulded. Thus it followed the pattern of education set by the colonizing nation, which quite often does not fit local conditions.

Types of Private Schools

This is important because of the sheer heterogeneity of the private sector in schooling, a heterogeneity which spans the entire range of scoio-economic categories in India as well as diverse religious and ethnic groups, and which extends to the nature of funding in these schools.

(a) Private Unaided (PUA) Schools

These schools are privately owned and funded, and rely, more or less, on user finance, unless they are schools which are run on philanthropic basis. Annual fees could range from Rs 100 to Rs. 50,000 or more, thus showing that they cover the entire socio-economic spectrum. Not so long ago this used to be considered an elitist sector, catering to the upper classes and offering a very expensive brand of education. But researches in recent years contradicts these impressions (Bashir, 1994, Kingdon 1996).

This sector was also thought to have a negligible presence, particularly in rural areas. Drawing on some primary survey evidence and challenging the reliability of the official education statistics, Kingdon (1996), among a handful of others, strongly contradicts the elitist picture of private schools. In broad outline, she suggests that official statistics, by excluding unrecognized schools from their enumeration, grossly underestimate the role of private sector, especially that of self financing schools in elementary education and that fee charging education is extremely heterogeneous, drawing its clientele from across the social spectrum. If private schools vary so widely as to be accessible to the highly privileged as well as some of those for less privileged, it seems logical to assume that schools may also range from the luxury class variant to the almost impoverished variant.

(b) Private Aided (PA) Schools

These schools are funded almost wholly (90-95%) by the government but management is private. In some States, the government sought the help of philanthropists to expand the educational system. In other States, philanthropists stepped in first and the government came in later. Basically, sponsors would provide the building and the facilities while the government meets staff salaries and some of the other recurring costs. The schools would benefit from the flexibility and accountability of private management while fees could be kept low enough for the poorer sections because of the government subsides in effect, a way of enlisting community support and management ensuring access to all income groups.

In the early decades after independence such philanthropists/charitable trusts did open aided schools, though these were generally in urban areas. The schools did great service in education and many such schools still continue to do so. Interestingly, in some of the educationally more advanced States like Kerala and Tamil Naidu, the aided school system has a strong presence. The aided school system dominates school education in Kerala managing nearly 60% of total schools at elementary level and accounts for 60% of expenditure by the State according to 1994-95 reports. In Tamil Naidu too, aided schools accounted for about 20% of elementary schools in 1993. The proportion is much higher for upper primary schools.

(c) Religious, Caste And Linguistic Schools

A large number of schools set up in the decades immediately before and after independence for providing educational facilities to particular caste, linguistic, or religious groups and fulfilled their promise with dedication. There are both aided and unaided schools with such orientation. Religious entrepreneurship has long been associated with private schooling and is trusted by adherents of that religion, and often even by members of the general public to propagate desired moral values/ cultural orientation. Fifty years after independence, schools run by Hindu religious orders like the Ramakrishna Mission as well as Muslim and Christian schools are very much in evidence. There are also schools run by other religious groups.

Many of these schools are aided. Within this sector too there is great heterogeneity and its size and scope are perhaps not fully understood. Religious minorities enjoy certain privileges under the law and have thus been able to avoid the problems of centralized recruitment, etc, which have begun to worry private aided schools in many States.

Rationale for Private Schooling

Nothing is ever done until everyone is convinced that it ought to be done, and has been convinced for so long that it is now time to do something else (Cornford, 1923). The controversies surrounding public education today have led some parents to resign themselves to the present situation. Others, concerned about the atmosphere in schools or the lack of learning they feel is taking place, have begun to teach their children at home or had shifted to private institutions. But at the same time these institutions fail to address the issues of mass education and compensatory education (one form of help for students who begin school with a deficit in terms of caste, socio-economic class or other social characteristics).

In our country, education is provided by the State as a matter of duty for all its citizens. The present statistics shows that the government is not fully able to fulfil its commitment. In certain circumstances, beyond doubt the private institutions are also contributing to the mission of "Education For All." But the dilemma is that the doors of private institutions are not open for all. This issue raises some crucial issues within the society, whether a large section of the society will remain deprived of a quality education, ultimately accentuating the class divide or education would pave the way for social equity.

The American sociologist Talcott Parsons (1950) argues that after primary socialization within the family, the school takes over as the focal socializing agency. The school acts as a bridge between the family and society as a whole, preparing the child for his adult role. It operates on meritocratic principles, status is achieved on the basis of merit. As society requires a highly motivated, achievement oriented workforce, this necessitates differential reward for differential achievement, a principle which has been established. Therefore, as a part of his process, it can be argued that there is no harm in utilizing the scarce resources of the State to provide quality education to at least a part of the society and try to gradually widen its base.

Like Parsons, Davis and Moore (1967) view education as a means of role allocation, but they link the educational system more directly with the system of social stratification. They see social stratification as a mechanism for ensuring that the most talented and able members of society are allocated to those positions which are functionally most important for society. Thus different types of educational system sift, sort and grade the individual in terms of his talent and abilities.

On the other hand, the Marxian view of the role of education is guided mostly by the issue of equality of opportunity in education. French sociologist Raymond Boudon (1974) agrees that inequality of educational opportunity is produced by a "two component process". The first component is the primary effect of stratification. It involves sub-cultural differences between social classes which are produced by the stratification system. The secondary effects stem simply from a person's actual position in the class structure. He maintains that even if there were no sub cultural differences between classes, the very fact that people start at different positions in the class system will produce inequality of educational opportunity such as the cost involved and the benefit to be gained.

From economic point of view, the American economists Bowles and Gintis (1976) agree that the fragmentation and compartmentalization of knowledge in school mirrors the organization of work in the economic system. The principle that differential attainment both produces and deserves differential record is firmly established in schools. Education legitimates inequality by creating the belief that schools provide the opportunity for fair and open competition where by talents and abilities are developed, graded and certificated. It is assumed that those students with good schooling receive the highest rewards. They further argue that educational and occupational attainment are related to the family back ground rather than talent and ability.

The effort of-a society which seeks to equalize opportunity, therefore, largely takes the form of providing services which compensate for the inequality in economic background through socialized community services and through provision of educational facilities. There are, of course, obvious difficulties in the providing such services and facilities adequately and universally. Not even the most developed countries would have the resources to provide it.

Moreover, so long as privately financed schools are allowed to exists along with the publicly financed schools it is difficult to achieve comparable quality in both types of schools. The private schools which are attended by children of the well-to-do offer better remuneration to their teachers, have smaller number of students in each class, provide better equipment and facilities. The publicly financed schools have to complete for funds with other activities of the State and the priority given to education is often not as high as the priority to irrigation, industry, roads, etc. The publicly financed schools, therefore, often compare unfavourably with the privately financed schools which cater to the upper income groups in society.

Present Scenario

Public expenditure on education in India was around Rs. 17,300 million in 1990-91 and accounted for 3.9% of the country's national income. Over the year public expenditure on education as a share of GNP has increased from 1.2% in 1950-51 to 3.9% in 1990-91. Despite this between 1986 and1994, the share of government school went down in almost all the States and in India as a whole. As a result the share of both government aided and private schools went up. When the increase in the share of aided and private schools is compared they are found to be generally higher in case of private schools than in the case of aided schools. It may be therefore, concluded that the growth in enrolment in private schools has been higher than in aided schools, possibly at the cost of government schools. This may be due to the availability of better facilities and teaching standards in private schools at the elementary level.

The proportion of children going to private schools according to NCAER report, 1999, is highest among the high income households, those in top segment of poverty classification, those who are salaried and professionals, as well as among the Muslims. It is interesting that over 70% of children from SC and ST households study in government schools. Only about 43% of Christian and 49% of Muslim children go both to government aided and private schools. This scenario suggests that government facilities cater to the requirements of the majority community in rural India. Lower participation of Muslim and Christian children in private schools may be related to both the medium of instruction and the content of curricula. Despite this first hand information, based mainly on local and traditional circumstances, the continuous decline in the functioning of government schools has generated a lot of demand for private schools in both rural as well as urban area and people from different strata of society irrespective of their class, caste and religion are sending their children to private schools.

There is wide variation between private schools in terms of service provided, level of fees, facilities available and so on. Some private schools are little more than coaching centres, run in a shack or a open space by some unemployed educated youth. Others have modern facilities, charge heavy fees, and try to project the image of a model school. At the same time, the empirical evidence, based on the mean scores of children in achievement tests, is not very conclusive. Some studies (Govinda and Varese, 1993, Kingdon, 1995) have shown that unaided private schools perform better than the government schools. Some other studies (Bashir, 1994) show that aided sector perform better than the unaided sector.

In most cases, private unaided schools enroll children from upper middle class families and that too after a series of selection tests. Needless to add, such a selection process segregates schools and children based on their capacity to pay and it accentuates social inequalities through educational process. It is interesting to note that the unaided sector survives and continues to expand despite the fact that the successive education policies have favoured a common school pattern for India. According to Fifth All India Education Survey, only 2% of students at primary level sought education in private schools in 1986. This increased to about 10% by 1994.

Private schooling is often thought to be confined to urban areas, but this is not the case. In many of the villages, private schools are a flourishing business. It presents both opportunities and dangers. Two conditions are favourable to the emergence of private schools in a specific area : (i) the dysfunctional government schools, and (ii) parental ability to pay.

With a view to explore the issues related with the role of private schooling and children in the context of Universalization of Elementary Education (U.E.E.) a study was conducted in a comparative framework in schools operating in rural and urban areas of two districts, Hazaribagh and West Singhbhum in the State of Jharkhand. In these two districts, one town and two rural blocks from each district were selected for study. In Hazaribagh, Barhi and Ichak blocks were selected where as in West Singhbhum, Chakradharpur and Gamharia blocks have been selected for the present study. Six schools each from the city and each of the blocks have been selected from one district. From one district the total number of selected schools were eighteen. Nine respondents from each school were chosen from parents, teachers and Secretaries of the private schools. Out of them, one is Secretary, three are teachers and five are guardians. Thus in both the districts, thirty six schools and 324 respondents were covered. The study broadly focussed on two objectives, viz, (i) Motivation of people in opening private schools and reasons for its increasing popularity, (ii) Teachers input, school environment and students performance.

To cope with the present challenge of universal primary education, many initiatives have been taken by the government, both at the central and the State level. Parallel to these efforts, a large number of private schools are also mushrooming both in rural and urban areas.

Table 1 : Educational level of school proprietors

Education	Total (%)
Matriculate	2.77
Intermediate	5.55
Graduate	52.77
Post Graduate	38.88

People who are taking initiative in opening private schools are well educated and this profession is attracting people from both the sexes. People who are in other profession also do not hesitate in opening private schools. Manifest reasons may be different but the ground level reality is that everyone who is involved in this affair finds it a easy way to make money. Some of these schools, for instance, are based on a mix of pecuniary and philanthropic motive. Sometimes an educated unemployed youth decides to set up an informal school, both to get some income as well as to contribute to the advancement of their village or community.

It is clear that the major motivation for opening a private school where the government primary school already existed did not appear to be a differentiated demand for innovative curriculum, or a community desire for a different linguistic or cultural orientation. Nor did it appear to be some kind of social service. The private schools are apparently responding to the unfulfilled demand for primary education since the government school system was largely dysfunctional.

One of the reasons for this scenario is that most of the primary schools suffer from various forms of infrastructural inadequacies and lack of required number of teachers. It was reported that about one third of the primary schools were single teacher schools (Govt. of India,1986). The teaching learning environment and quality are so unsatisfactory that teachers themselves would arrange for their own children's education in better run schools. The elite and the rich in the villages also have started avoiding government primary schools and getting their wards better education in private schools. Ultimately, the stakeholders of these schools being weak and vulnerable can not ensure accountability of the system for quality education, since interests of their children's education are safe in private schools.

Table 2 : Profession of guardians

Profession	Frequency (%)
Service	46.66
Business	35.55
Agriculture	7.22
Private Service	2.22
Housewife	8.33

Guardian's profession does not determine the choice of schools. Guardians with diverse education levels and professions are interested in quality education which in their opinion the government schools have failed to provide. Similarly the monthly income of the guardians does not inhibit them for sending their children to a private school. Guardians demand for private schooling is mainly raising due to inadequate infrastructure in government school and teacher input.

Table 3: Reasons for sending children to private schools

Reasons	Frequency (%)
Good education	87.88
Declining quality of government school	87.77
Good discipline	86.66
Status symbol	78.88
Proper care of students	74.44
English medium	71.66
Good atmosphere of school	61.66
Qualified teachers	57.22
C.B.S.E. syllabus	48.88

There is an interesting inter-relationship between parental perception of private schools and their support for the schooling of their children. Parents on the whole, seemed clear that their children would benefit much more from private schooling. Guardians had an preference for private schooling due to following reasons:

(a) Something which will help the children complete secondary education and get a job in organized sector.

(b) Knowledge of English which may help the child get admission into English medium government/ aided schools at the next level.

(c) Advanced Math/Science which is useful for professional courses.

(d) Providing an alternative in the poor quality government schools and building the child gain in intangibles such as learning how to study, rise in self confidence and self esteem, with a view to transfer him to government / aided school later.

Parents can only assess private schools in terms of active teaching level, there are other parameters which are less obvious, especially at the lower level. One aspect would definitely be teacher's competence and teacher experience. A second would be difficulty in assessing in what exactly is happening in the school.

However, the main advantage of private schools is being more accountable. They have higher levels of teaching activity. English medium instruction is a big selling point of private schools. Generally, the rapport between the guardians and the teachers is more constructive in private schools than in government schools.

Posters, hoarding and pamphlets are the best publicity device used in this profession. As in other professions, the private school too face challenge from their rival and here the role of publicity becomes significant. Selection method based on test is only used by certain schools who have some reputation in society over the years. Once the reputation is established, they have the option to reject and select the students which as a matter of fact again provides them the credibility of being a quality school. Schools which are new, strive for a reputation in the market and seldom take the risk of conducting an admission test. Their motto is maximum enrolment. But the crucial problem faced by many private schools is that it is hard for them to obtain official recognition from the government. Without recognition, private schools cannot issue recognised primary school certificates.

Tuition fee and other charges are high in private schools in comparison to government schools. Despite this the attraction for sending the children in private schools is gradually increasing. Even among poor families and disadvantaged communities one finds guardians who make great sacrifices to send some or all their children to private schools. The reason, almost invariably, is that they are dissatisfied with the functioning of local government schools.

About half of the teachers in the sampled schools were women. Most of the teachers were graduate. Women from middle class families join this profession to keep themselves busy. For them earning from this profession is not so important. But for others, the salary which they get is almost one fourth of their counterparts in government schools. At the same time their commitment is almost double as compared to government school. The management of private schools are exploiting the mass unemployed manpower on the pretext of providing job opportunity.

Teachers are kept engaged during six hours school time. Everyone is expected to perform best in the interest of the school. Keeping the students engaged and performing regular activities is the biggest skill required to be successful as a teacher in the private school.

In private schools the efficiency of the teacher is determined by his ability to keep the students involved in one or more classroom activities. They are under a strong pressure, since they might lose their job if attendance declines due to poor teaching standard. Thus in private schools teachers have little reasons to promote the personal development of the children, to treat them with sensivity, or to impart a sense of value. Their prime objective is to prepare the students to pass the relevant tests and examination.

If we look at teacher - student ratio and teacher qualification, both aspects of quality in school infrastructure, the evidence is varied. Certainly the private schools had a better student - teacher ratio than government schools. Even multi-grade teaching, though common was different. Since classes were smaller, it was obviously not as problematic. It was rare to find one teacher handling all five classes as we found in some government schools. However, teaching skills for primary level children were not superior to those found among government school teachers. Only some teachers had professional pre-service training. It is here that private schools fared very badly. As for in service training this was a rarity in these schools.

Parent - teachers meetings are frequent in private schools. Generally this opportunity is used by the teachers to ask the guardians for arranging tuition for

Table 4 : Reasons for good performance of private schools

Reasons	Frequency
Good discipline	21.29
Use of modern TLM	21.29
English medium instruction	19.44
Regular test	15.74
Separate teachers for different subjects	12.96
Adequate infrastructure	11.11
Attention to each student	7.40
Efficient management	6.48
Limited number of students	5.55

Findings of the Study

Because of irregular attendance, repetition and drop-out, in addition to low enrolment in the first grade of primary schools, only a small proportion of children is able to complete primary education. The fact that many of the children in primary schools, particularly in rural areas never goes beyond the lowest grades suggests that primary schooling is less effective than might be assumed by simply considering the enrolment rates. Legislation dealing with compulsory education would seem to testify to the interest of the government in improving school attendance and retention rates. But the responsibility of parents for keeping their children in school has not become a firm part of the mores and no administration is prepared to enforce, laws that could radically change these norms.

Table 1: NPRC-wise extent of drop-out

NPRC	Total Students	Total Dropout	% of Dropout	% of Male	% of Female	% of General	% of SC	% of OBC
1.	579	155	26.77	47.74	52.25	0.64	77.41	21.93
2.	997	8	0.80	75.00	25.00	-	37.50	62.50
3.	680	173	25.44	47.39	52.60	5.78	60.69	33.52
4.	605	189	31.23	51.85	48.14	1.05	65.07	33.88
5.	655	32	4.88	55.00	50.00	21.87	37.50	40.62
6.	440	13	2.95	46.15	53.84	-	7.69	92.30
7.	358	29	8.14	51.72	48.27	-	6.89	93.10
8.	893	28	3.13	46.42	53.57	10.71	17.85	71.42
Grand Total	5205	627	12.04	49.55	50.45	9.80	19.60	70.58

Out of the total students who got enrolled in Class I in the year 1996, about 12.04% did not complete their five years of primary schooling and became drop-out. Among them female students had a larger concentration. Caste-wise classification reveals that children belonging to OBC category have greater tendency to leave the school without completing their five years of schooling.

Table 2 : Gender wise drop-out students in comparison to exist class

Class	Male	Female	Total
Class I	45.45	54.54	7.01
Class II	45.33	54.66	23.92
Class III	42.49	57.40	34.44
Class IV	56.32	43.67	25.19
Class V	69.49	30.50	9.40

Maximum number of students left the school after two years i.e. in Class III. This was followed by the students who left in Class IV and Class II respectively. The data indicates that the lowest number of student left school before completing their one year education. This proves that the schooling system, school infrastructure and teacher's attitude play a vital role in retaining the students throughout five years of primary education. It seems that parents willingness to send their children in school has increased but the school atmosphere is not fully conducive to retain them throughout five years.

Table 3 : NPRC-wise extent of transfer

NPRC	% of Total Transfer	% of Male Transfer	% of Female Transfer	% of General Transfer	% of SC Transfer	% of OBC Transfer
1.	5.69	81.81	18. 18	-	60.60	39.40
2.	44.93	50.66	49.33	12.27	33.48	54.24
3.	22.50	65.53	34.64	12.41	52.94	34.64
4.	13.70	63.85	36.14	6.02	60.24	33.73
5.	67.78	59.68	40.31	14.63	59.54	35.81
6.	53.18	48.71	51.28	25.21	17.52	57.26
7.	46.34	53.93	46.06	10.90	20.00	69.69
8.	37.62	52.98	47.91	4.46	22.02	73.51
Total	36.42	53.37	46.62	12.44	35.28	52.26

On the whole 36.42% students from the COHORT obtained transfer from their respective schools in different years. Sexwise classification reveals that male students outnumber female students on the issue of school transfer. The figure is very high if we compare it with the figures of drop-out students. It was observed during the study that the school administration had no knowledge about the where about of the students who left school and were categorised as 'transfer case' in the school document. Whether they are continuing their studies in other government schools or in other privately managed schools is difficult to conclude. Situation like this sometimes indicate that many of the transfer case may be a genuine dropout which had been concealed by the school authorities on the pretext of transfer to save themselves from the anger of their superior. This is a new development in the field of primary education in some recent years to hide the actual figure of dropout at every level at the cost of other excuse.

Table 4 : Class-wise transfer of students

Class	Male	Female	Total
Class I	42.30	57.69	2.99
Class II	49.21	50.78	10.07
Class III	60.38	39.61	27.68
Class IV	54.17	45.82	43.61
Class V	56.14	43.85	15.87
Grand Total	53.37	46.62	36.42

As discussed earlier this study reveals a low rate of dropout among the surveyed schools but at the same time the ratio of transfer is quite high. Most of the reported transfer case was in Class IV and here female students outnumbered male students where as the overall transfer rate among male students is comparatively high. Even in Class I and Class V transfer case of students was reported. It is very easy for the school administration to declare any student who has left the school due to any reason as transfer case to escape their responsibility to bring back the children in school through persuading their parents for the same. One of the objectives of the DPEP is that the school administration is responsible to see that all the school going age children in its catchment area are in school, but findings like this ridicule this idea for Universalization of Elementary Education.

Table 5 : NPRC-wise retention of students at primary level

NPRC	Total Student	Total Survival	Male Survival	Female Survival
1.	579	29.53	71.92	28.07
2.	997	27.88	46.01	53.98
3.	680	13.52	63.04	36.95
4.	605	16.19	63.26	36.73
5.	655	18.01	46.61	53.38
6.	440	22.04	52.57	47.42
7.	356	34.55	56.91	43.08
8.	893	26.98	41.07	58.92
Total	2344	25.46	46.06	53.94

Altogether the survival rate was 25.46% for the students in the eight NPRC of two districts covered under the present study. Among the boys, out of the total survival who completed their five years of primary education without any interruption, the survival rate is 46.06, some what lower than female survival rate.

Table 6: Educational status of guardians of drop-out students

Education	Frequency
Illiterate	76.71
Primary	4.79
Middle	12.32
Secondary	4.79
Intermediate	1.36
B.A. and Above	-

Majority of dropout children's parents were illiterate. This shows that most of the drop-out children are first generation learners. Neither themselves nor their guardians are keen to attain education. This apathy is especially prevalent in rural areas. More deeply rooted is the prejudice against educating girls. Another hurdle may be described as 'alienation'. Some parents simply feel that the schooling system is not for them. This feeling can arise in various ways. There may be no tradition or culture of schooling in their caste or community. The teacher may treat them with indifference, contempt or even hostility. Their children may be discriminated at school. For these and other reasons, some parents conclude that it is better to stay away.

It was also noticed that parents find the cost of schooling high. The most expensive item is clothing, followed by textbooks and stationary. Most of the parents cannot afford annual expenditure. They are often constrained to produce cash at short notice to meet immediate needs. In many families, the education of daughters is treated as an expendable item, easily renounced if a financial difficulty arises. The perceived lack of economic return contributes a great deal to this attitude when the household finds itself unable to send all the children to school, the tendency is to give priority to boys.

Table 7: Efforts made by government to increase enrolment according to teachers

Response	Frequency
Provision for books	91.97
Provision for mid-day meal	91.57
Provision for scholarship	89.47
Improvement in infrastructure	31.57
Maintenance of teacher - student ratio	16.84

Provision of mid-day meal and free distribution of books are the major efforts made by the government to increase enrolment and retention among the school going age children. Proper distribution of scholarship has also encouraged the students of deprived communities to retain in school throughout five years. Problem of poor infrastructure has been overcome to a great extent under DPEP and Operation Black Board programme in almost every part of the State.

Intervention has been made to make adequate arrangements of class rooms, toilets, drinking water facility, chair and table in the school. Teachers also reported that retention of students in school becomes difficult once the mid-day meal gets discontinued.

Table 8 : Response regarding discontinuation of children education according to parents

Response	Frequency
Poor economic condition	100.00
Poor quality of education	41.91
Not interested in education	31.61
Government assistance not on time	2.20
Teachers are unfriendly	0.73

Almost all parents hold the view that the poor economic condition of the family is the main reason for child to become a drop-out. About 41.91% parents were of the opinion that the school does not provide quality education and therefore, the students do not find the education interesting, resulting in dropout.

Slow progress at school is also one of the main causes of parental frustration. Many children are still unable to read after several years of schooling. This picture of dismal pupil achievement, especially in deprived areas persists. This disincentive is also common in under-privileged families. The frustration of non-functioning school, for instance, are particularly hard to bear for those who cannot afford private tuition and are unable to create a learning environment at home. Similarly first generation learners and their parents are highly vulnerable to this discouragement effect. Illiterate parents often find it difficult to judge what goes on in the classroom.

Parents also find justification for keeping their children out of school in many of the long established traditions and circumstances of living. A major justification is the economic condition of the family. Children traditionally participated in work at even a tender age, they are regarded as a reserve pool of labour. The greater usefulness of girls in performing domestic tasks may be one of the reasons why the figures of their enrolment and attendance at school are smaller than those for boys. Even if they enter primary schools, after some years of schooling, custom and the need to keep girls at home with the house work and look after younger children result in considerable wastage among girl pupils. This attitude tends to be more rigid in rural areas where overall girls either did not go to school or drop out because of a combination of economic reasons and compulsions of responsibilities at home.

Table 9 : Guardian's response regarding desired change in schooling system

Response	Frequency
Scholarship amount should be increased	100.00
Arrangement of mid-day meal and books	72.05
Facility for remedial education	34.55
Teachers should come on time	25.73
Teaching standard should be improved	13.97

Almost all the parents were of the view that scholarship amount should be raised. At present it fails to meet the required educational expenses of a students. In some schools it was noticed that teachers, mostly young, conducted an innovative experiment at their own level by forcing the parents to prepare school dress from scholarship money. Such efforts bring discipline but still its area of operation is limited. From this point of view, hike in scholarship amount is justifiable. It should be linked to attendance.

Table 10 : Shortcoming on the part of government to eradicate the problems of drop-out according to teachers

Response	Frequency
No alternative for child labour	67.36
Lack of will power	29.47
Lack of infrastructure	25.26
Any other	10.52

Arrangement of more alternative school is also an important issue raised by the teachers.

The problem of child labour has a direct impact on the schooling of children. Still all schools do not have adequate infrastructure to provide quality education to all children. The gradual improvement in the quality of life of a large chunk of population in rural areas, belonging to all communities and side by side their exposure to urban areas through personal visits and due to the vast electronic revolution in rural areas has raised their expectation from the system of education.

In most of the schools facilities available are minimal. Teaching material are limited to textbooks, slates and some basic textbooks. The pathetic physical condition of few schools is in sharp contrast with the claims recently made by the government under DPEP programme.

But at the same time under the DPEP programme efforts are being made to tackle certain schools were the number of teachers are less. In this direction appointment of Shiksha Mitra are being made so that the school can run on time and proper teaching is imparted. Proper teaching of students on time and distribution of government assistance has a major role to play in decreasing the rate of dropout and increasing retention. DPEP programme is doing some positive work in this direction and has achieved substantial improvement in the existing condition.

Overview

Significant efforts have been made in the last fifty years to universalize primary education. Across the country, educational facilities are now available to a large segment of population. The enrolment at the primary level of education over time had improved significantly but still some section of the society are out of school. More important is the problem of maximum retention and the existence of dropout. Although the figures of dropout has decreased in some recent years due to the impact of DPEP and government sponsored incentive schemes to an extent.

Retention is closely related to the enrolment and many factors that have emerged and calls for interventions to increase the holding power of the school or of the non-formal education system. While talking to such parents whose children have dropped out of the school system it emerged that some parents do not want education for their children as it alienates them from their social setup. There is need to decentralize the educational curriculum planning on the pattern of Madhya Pradesh to suit the job requirements of the local community.

The suitability of school timing and retention needs further probe and in a more scientific manner. As of now, from the data available, it is rather difficult to say that it has some relationship. At the same time it is a matter of common knowledge that it was a significant factor convenient to the out of school children.

There is a definite case for launching the awareness campaign about the incentive schemes especially among those parents whose children are not going to the school. Further investigations are also required to find out the reasons for the drop-out children not wanting to come back to the school system.

The education of girls is significantly influenced by mother's literacy level as well by schooling factors. In the context of less developed regions and backward population, literate mothers and good schools are strong incentives to enrolment and retention of children in school.

Absence of preschool facilities and drop-out have some kind of relationship. The extension of preschools emerges to be a prime need. Linkages with other organization like I.C.D.S. may be fruitful.

The study has provided sufficient evidence that serious inequalities in literacy and educational opportunities among regions and caste groups, and between sex exists. In order to remove the inequalities between educationally backward and advanced villages within the same district, local specific educational programmes and policies should be formulated and implemented with active local participation.

Village Education Committees have not been actively participating in the affairs of the schools in most of the areas. It is expected that with the establishment/ Constitution of the Panchayats under the new Constitutional provisions, these would become effective, but it would be desirable to chalk out the role and functions of these Village Education Committees in a manner that accountability of the education functionaries is ensured.

References

Aggarwal, Y. (1999) : Trends in Access And Retention, National Institute of Educational Planning and Administration, New Delhi.

Ambasht, N. K. & Rath, K. B. (1995) : A Study of the Effect of Household, Community and School Factors on the Enrolment, Retention and Achievement of Scheduled Tribe Children at Primary Level, Indian Educational Review, National Council of Educational Research And Training, Vol. 30, No. 1, New Delhi, January - 1995.

Anandalakshmy, S. (1999) : Public Report on Basic Education in India, Oxford University Press, New Delhi.

Banerji, R. (1997) : Why don't Children Complete Primary Education, Economic And Political Weekly, Vol-XXXII, No. 32, Agust 9-15.

Debi, Sailabala (2001) : Inequality of Access to Elementary Education in Orissa : An Inter and Intra - Spatial Analysis, in Vaidyanathan, A. and P. R. Gopinathan Nair (eds), Primary Education in Rural India : A Grassroots View, Sage Publications, New Delhi.

Hassan, Arif (1997) : School Drop-outs And The Myth of Child Labour, Exchanges, Issue No. 18, September 1997, Banglore.

Kumar, N. (et. al) (2002) : A Study of Enrolment, Retention, Drop-out and Completion Rate in Primary Schools of Two DPEP Districts, Sulabh Institute of Development Studies, Patna.

Majumdar Manabi (2001) : Educational Opportunities in Rajasthan and Tamil Nadu : Despair and Hope, in Vaidyanathan, A and P. R. Gopinathan Nair (eds), Primary Education in Rural India : A Grassroots View, Sage Publications, New Delhi.

Myrdal, G. (1992) : Asian Drama, Kalyani Publishers, New Delhi.

Papola, T.S. (1998) : Elementary Education in India, Giri Institute of Social Sciences, Lucknow.

UNFPA (1997) : Towards Population And Development Goals, Oxford University Press, New Delhi.

5

ACADEMIC FACILITATION AT NATIONAL INSTITUTE OF OPEN SCHOOLING STUDY CENTRES

NIRAJ KUMAR

Introduction

Open learning is one of most rapidly growing aspects of education and training in the world today. The potential impact of distance learning on all education delivery systems, from the primary to secondary level, has been greatly accentuated through new developments in information and communication technologies which increasingly free learners from the constraints of time and space.

In pursuance of the National Policy on Education and its commitment to attain Universalization of Elementary Education For All, the Govt. of India has been exploring all possible mechanisms and alternatives, besides the formal schooling system and the Non-formal education through the National Literacy Mission, Open schooling system has also come into being as a viable alternative. It intends to provide opportunity for continuing and life oriented education to persons of all ages with particular focus on (a) children who are school drop-outs and non starters and (b) adults who are either illiterate or attained literacy under the programme of National Literacy Mission.

In India the idea of Open schooling was first conceived in the early 70s. In August 1974, a working group was appointed by the NCERT to examine the feasibility of setting up an Open school. It was recognised that the country was facing a persistent problem of school drop-outs. It was, therefore, felt that it was in the interest of both the dropouts as well as of the nation that they be accorded an opportunity of come back to the mainstream and continue their education. The problem of education of girls and children belonging to rural and economically backward communities also deserved special attention and it was realised that unless an Open Learning System (OLS) was provided for, where the children as well as adults could take advantage of the opportunities for education at their own convenience and at their own place, it would continue to pose a very difficult problem.

Thus in 1987-88, the Department of Education, Ministry of Human Resource Development, initiated the preparation of a project report for the establishment of National Open School(N.O.S.), as an autonomous registered society, which was accepted by the government on November 23, 1989. In 1990, N.O.S was vested with the authority of conducting secondary and Senior Secondary examinations and certification there of and a gazette notification in this regard was published on October 20, 1990. The Central Board of Secondary Education which was the certifying and examining authority on behalf of N.O.S. then ceased to be so with effect from 20th October 1990. Under this authority N.O.S. conducted its first Secondary and Senior Secondary examinations all over India in January 1991 for about 35,000 students. And a decade later in the year 2002, N.O.S. became N.I.O.S. (National Institute of Open Schooling) and further broaden its area of operation.

The National Institute of Open Schooling reaches out to unreached sections of society which includes school drop-outs and marginalised groups such as rural youth, urban poor, girls and women, scheduled castes and scheduled tribes, backward classes, handicapped persons and ex-servicemen. It has on its roll students and learners from almost every State and Union Territory of India and some centres outside the country. This indicates the popularity of its services.

The National Institute of Open Schooling designs its own curriculum, prepare instructional materials in print and electronic modes, conduct examinations and certify students upto pre-degree level. It provides the following programmes (a) Foundation Course, (b) Secondary Education Course, (c) Senior Secondary Course, (d) Open Basic Education for Universal Elementary Education, (e) Life Enrichment Course, and (f) Vocational Education Courses.

The programmes of NIOS are offered through Distance Education Mode (DEM) which comprises the following : (i) Printed Self Learning Materials, prepared by the academic staff of the NIOS, (ii) Audio and Video programmes developed by Media Unit and made available to the study centres (iii) National Telecast on Doordarshan (DD-1) and Gyan Darshan, (iv) Personal Contact Programme (PCPs) that is through classes, tutorials and counselling organized in selected recognised schools and institutions referred to as Accredited Institutions or study centres, (v) Interactive Quarterly Magazine called 'Open Learning' serving as printed tutorial. The NIOS has also strengthened the area of elementary education by striking a partnership with N.G.Os. by providing them prototype material for adaptation, helping them with materials development workshops, providing them blueprints for examination papers and standards and providing joint certification.

The NIOS attempts to provide education to students near their place of stay or work with flexibility of time, place and choice of subjects with the aim to suit their convenience and interest. Students can choose their subjects of their study in consultation with the Co-ordinators of the Accredited Institutions (AIS) or study centres. Students are allowed and encouraged to choose vocational subjects in combination with academic subjects at both Secondary and Senior Secondary levels. Vocational courses can be taken in Accredited Vocational Institutions (AVIs). The NIOS has also Accredited Institutions called Special Accredited Institutions for Education of the Disadvantaged (SAIED) to cater to the needs of people with physical and mental disabilities, the socially and geographically isolated and disadvantaged sections such as street children, working children, rural women, scheduled castes and scheduled tribes. Academic courses like Open Basic Education, Secondary and Senior Secondary courses and Vocational courses are being offered independently or in combination with academic subject through SAIED.

One of the distinctive features of NIOS is that there is provision for two full scale examinations every year, one in May and the other in October. The student has the option to appear in one or more subjects of one's choice or take them all together. In case of failure, one can appear again, within the five year period. All passes are kept as credits and when the student has acquired the required number of credits, the certificate is issued.

Recently NIOS has introduced an examination scheme called Examination On Demand. Its approach of examination is totally different from that of the formal system. A student can appear for the examination of any class round the year without producing any proof of earlier passed exam. It is a boon for the students residing in remote area where there are shortage of formal schools. At present one centre each with this facility is in operation in Bihar and Jharkhand. Very soon some more centres of NIOS will have this examination facility at their centres.

The NIOS established a number of Regional Centres for proper functioning of open schooling system. A regional centre has a large number of study centres under its control. Since it is not possible for the Regional Centre individually to monitor and supervise

adequately the functioning of each study centre, there is a provision of appointing Academic Facilitators to facilitate the functioning of the study centres in the region.

Facilitators are academicians serving or retired or educational administrators of the area who provide their expertise for the benefit of the staff of the study centre and the students attached with them. For quality control an Academic Facilitator is given the responsibility of one study centre. He is required to pay 10 to 12 visits at crucial junctures to make their visit fruitful. The main responsibilities of Facilitators are (i) to provide quality services to the students, (ii) to monitor the functioning of the study centres regularly to assure quality, (iii) to provide academic support to the tutors and the students at the centre, (iv) to respond to the students need and grievances, and help in resolving their problems connected with admission, supply of study materials, change of subjects, issue of data sheet, identity cards, mark-sheets, migration certificates, pass certificates, etc. (v) to build a systematic channel of communication between the national, regional and study centres level, (vi) to liaise continuously with NIOS to update oneself with the latest amendments in the rules and regulations for admission, personal contact programme, assignments, examination, certificate etc and (vii) to report to NIOS and Regional centre in order to provide insight into the actual problems of the study centres so that adequate steps can be taken to resolve the problems.

Types of NIOS Institutions

(a) Accredited Institutions (AI)

The National Open School approves certain organizations from different places and gives authority (accredition) to them to act as study centres as well as to perform all such functions as required under rules framed by it. A memorandum of understanding is signed by both the parties. Accredited institutions are generally those Secondary and Senior Secondary schools and other teaching institutions which are recognised by the Central or State Governments. In exceptional cases, registered societies having a good record of work are also chosen for study centres. However, accredition is given after rigorous screening of application on the basis of prescribed criteria and after inspection of the institution by a committee of experts.

An Accredited Institution (hereinafter referred as AI) as a catalytic agent of NIOS has to perform the following functions:

1. To publicize the opportunities offered by NIOS for pursuing different categories of school education and other relevant information.
2. To provide prospectus and admission forms to intended students.
3. To provide counselling to students in the choice of subjects of study.
4. To register the students for the courses during the specified periods.
5. To distribute reading materials to the students.
6. To arrange classes or Personal Contact Programmes for students and to ensure that the classes are held as per the announced routines.
7. To ensure safe custody and proper use of teaching aids and equipments supplied by the NIOS.
8. To provide library and laboratory facilities to the students.
9. To conduct through teachers and tutors assessment of required number of assignments of students and send their records to NIOS.
10. To ensure that examination forms/fees are received and sent to NIOS on time.
11. To distribute data sheet, mark sheet and other certificates to the students.

12. To provide school premises for conducting NIOS examinations, if required by NIOS.

(b) Accredited Vocational Institutions (AVI)

The National Open School offers vocational education to the target groups through accredited vocational institutions in addition to general and academic courses. It offers vocational courses upto pre-degree level in the broad areas of Agriculture, Engineering and Technology, Health and Paramedical, Home Science, Computer Science and Information Technology, Library and Information Science, Business and Commerce, Secretarial practice, and other vocational and life enrichment areas.

The vocational education courses are broadly divided into two categories (a) package course and (b) stand alone vocational subjects/course. A package course consists of two or more modules/papers/ subjects. The duration of a package course varies from six months to more than two years. On completion of a package course, certificate or Diploma is awarded depending upon the nature and duration of the course. Some of the package courses offered by NIOS are Secretarial practice, Radiography, Library Science, Early Childhood Care and Education, Computer Application, Plumbing, T.V. repairing, Dress making and Refrigeration and Air Conditioning.

Stand alone vocational subjects/courses are undertaken independently as a vocational course or in combination with academic subjects. Some of the standalone subjects are Type Writing, Word Processing, Carpentry, Solar Energy Technology, Bio-Technology, Catering Management, Poultry farming, Welding Technology, and Soil and Fertilizer Management. The credit earned on passing the stand alone subject can be combined with the credits of four academic subjects for the purpose of certification.

NIOS vocational programms have certain distinctive

features. Unlike formal education system, NIOS allows freedom to learn and acquire skills at one's own pace. A student can take examination in different modules one by one or together over a period of five years from the date of registration. Secondly, in courses having more than one module a student can appear and pass in one or more modules at a time. The pass credit or credits earned can be accumulated till he passes all the modules in that course and is awarded the certificate. Like general academic courses, vocational courses are imparted through open learning mode which comprises three basic elements : (a) Self learning printing materials, (b) Video programme and (c) Personal Contact Programme (PCPs).

(c) Special Accredited Institutions for Education of the Disadvantaged (SAIED)

The NIOS has special accredited institutions called Special Accredited Institutions for Education of the Disadvantaged to provide both academic and vocational courses to physically and socially disadvantaged groups of people. These special institutions cater to the needs of the people with physical and mental disabilities, the socially and geographically isolated and disadvantaged sections such as street children, working children, rural women, the Scheduled castes and the Scheduled tribes. In this, academic courses like Open Basic Education, Secondary and Senior Secondary courses and Vocational courses are offered independently or in combination with academic subject.

Earlier Researches in Distance Education and Open Schooling

In India, systematic attempts to study the various aspects of distance education began in 1976. Mukhopadhy and Sujatha (1998) and Sahoo (1990) have analysed the researches done in the field of distance education in India.

One of the major constituents of distance education system is the method of giving assignments to the learners. It acts as a major device for providing feedback to the students in order to support their learning process. The national level studies conducted by Biswal (1981) and Mouley (1986) revealed that most of the students, who received evaluated assignments on time, favoured the system of compulsory submission of assignments and findings were supported by the research works carried out by Sahoo in 1985 and Kumar in 1986. Similar results were reported by Matiosam (1971) who summarized a large number of researches done on the subject of effectiveness of assignments in distance education system of U.S.A.

Another important aspect related to the system of assignments is their turn around time. It refers to the time taken by the distance education to send back the evaluated response sheets to the students. This aspect was taken into account in the studies conducted by Singh (1988), Sahoo (1985), Mouley (1986) and Balasubramanium (1986). These research findings were unanimous on the conclusion that there exist a general lack of promptness among distance education organizations in dispatching evaluated response sheets to their respective students. According to Nagaraju (1982) and Sahoo (1985), the distance education institutes rarely took interest in resolving the doubts of students regarding the question posed in assignments. Another study conducted by Biswal in 1979, revealed that the students expressed their desire for more elaborated comments on the assignments so as to provide them the requisite feedback in this regard.

In India, both micro level and macro level studies have been conducted to measure the effectiveness of one or more aspects of distance education system. A large contribution has been made by Koul, Vaydehi, Sarwal and Sahoo by carrying out micro level studies in this field. These studies have looked at the intricate relationships of influential factors in a singular institute's working and have provided useful information regarding effective decision in making a programme developed for self learning. The macro - level researches conducted by Mouley, Dutt, Gupta and Biswal are rich in data and have provided valuable findings related to different aspects of distance education system as structure, planning and controlling of academic activities, development and distribution of course materials, submission of student response sheets, conducting examinations, organizing the personal contact prograammes, etc.

Relevance and Objectives

This study is important for understanding the prevailing environment in the NIOS institutions and the nature of interaction between the institutions and the students. It is also relevant for improving the functioning of the institutions and for enlarging the canvas of Open School System in India. Thus this study is broadly based on four objectives, viz. (i) To find out infrastructural facilities available in the institution (ii) To examine the academic environment in the institutions through analysing academic support structure including Personal Contact Programme (PCP) , (iii) To identify the factors promoting or hindering the spread of NIOS system, and (iv) To suggest remedial measures for more efficient functioning of the NIOS.

The study has been conducted in the States of Bihar and Jharkhand in all the institutions accredited by NIOS. A sample was drawn consisting of 15 students and 5 teachers from every functional institution for detailed study. Thus a sample of 741 persons from the two States comprising of 500 Open school students, 195 teachers and 46 centres Co-ordinators, were interviewed with a set of schedules. Besides, the Regional Director, NIOS, Patna, was also contacted with an interview guide.

Findings of the Study

(a) Accredited Institutions (AI)

Table 1 : Occupation and caste of guardians

Occupation	Bihar				Jharkhand				
	General	OBC	SC	Total	General	OBC	SC	ST	Total
Labour	-	-	0.7	0.7	-	-	2.0	-	2.0
Agriculture	8.9	2.2	-	11.2	-	1.4	9.6	0.7	11.6
Business	29.8	7.5	0.7	38.0	39.0	6.2	0.7	1.4	47.2
Service	41.8	6.0	2.2	50.0	25.3	2.0	10.3	1.4	39.0
Total	80.6	15.7	3.7	100.0	64.4	9.6	22.6	3.4	100.0

It is evident that facility of NIOS is confined to upper and backward castes. On the whole the Scheduled castes and Scheduled tribes students are yet to derive full benefit of Open school. It is also evident that those who are in service and business have sent their wards to open schools. Thus it is mainly socially and economically advantaged sections of the population that have been deriving benefit from open schooling.

Table 2 : Reasons for admission in Accredited Institutions

Reasons	Bihar	Jharkhand	Total
Admission difficulty in formal school	20.9	15.1	17.8
Time saving	5.2	30.1	18.2
Suitability of school hours	9.7	12.3	11.1
Simple study materials	20.1	16.4	18.2
No age bar	13.4	6.2	9.6
Useful for dropouts	8.9	5.5	7.1
Useful for girls	10.4	5.5	7.8
Less expensive	11.2	8.9	10.0

It is found that reasons for admission in open school are many. But a sizeable number of them think that admission in formal schools is not as easy as in open schools. Availability of study materials, timing of

Personal Contact Programme, time relaxation in passing the examination are the other major reasons for their admission. Open school is also considered to be useful for girls, less expensive and useful for drop-out students. Hence reasons for opting for admission are numerous and no single reason can be spotted out as the most important one.

Table 3 : Information about NIOS courses

Reasons	Bihar	Jharkhand	Total
Newspaper	17.2	2.8	9.6
Friends	22.4	30.9	26.8
School Management	40.2	43.1	41.8
Guardian	13.5	4.8	8.9
Regional Office	4.5	3.4	3.9
Others	2.2	15.0	9.0

It is evident that major source of information regarding NIOS courses, admission and other matters is the study centre. Next important source is their friends. Since the major agencies of information dissemination are study centres and friends or interpersonal contact, information about NIOS courses does not seem to be available in far flung areas. People adjoining the study centres only are aware of it.

Notwithstanding, whether or not awareness about NIOS system has percolated down to the remote areas and among the underprivileged groups of the people. Most of the Co-ordinators claim that advertisement about NIOS system is made by the study centres. However, the officials, claims that more efforts remain to be made to popularize Open schooling in the villages of the two States. Posters, charts and other campaign techniques need to be used for creating awareness among the rural people and motivating the disadvantaged section of society for availing the opportunity.

However, the NIOS make efforts to provide necessary information about admission and other related aspects on Open schooling. This is endorsed by the bulk of the students.

Table 4 : Availability of facilities at Accredited Institutions

Items	Students		Co-ordinators	
	Bihar	Jharkhand	Bihar	Jharkhand
Laboratory	95.0	46.0	100.0	100.0
Library	65.0	57.0	100.0	100.0
Classroom	100.0	100.0	100.0	100.0
Furniture	100.0	100.0	100.0	100.0
Drinking water	100.0	100.0	100.0	100.0
Toilet for boys	100.0	100.0	100.0	100.0
Toilet for girls	100.0	100.0	100.0	100.0
Play ground	81.0	63.0	100.0	100.0
Electricity	100.0	100.0	100.0	100.0
Audio-visual equipments	49.0	46.0	86.0	100.0

Although there are much similarity in their responses, a sizeable number of students do not agree that in all the study centres, there is library, laboratory, audio-visual equipments and play grounds. More students in Jharkhand than in Bihar reported the shortage of these facilities in the study centres. Some Co-ordinators admit that their schools do not have audio - visual equipment.

Considering the importance of the opinion of both the parties (students and Coordinators) regarding the availability of facilities at AIs, it is essential to make an observation about the views of two. The students who are the suffering party always reported the actual fact but the Co-ordinators on the other hand concealed many facts on the pretext of their institution reputation. Thus the views of the students on such issues pretend to be more reliable.

Personal Contact Programme (PCP) in NIOS is a mechanism through which the process of face to face interaction between teachers and students is operationalized. In PCP classes, students get the opportunity to interact with fellow students and teachers to resolve the difficulties in comprehending the study materials. These classes also enable them to pursue their study more seriously. Hence PCP forms the hub of the NIOS scheme.

Table 5 Teaching methods in Personal Contact Programme

Methods	Bihar	Jharkhand
Lecture	67.9	56.2
Demonstration	29.1	28.0
Laboratory	24.6	10.3
Group Discussion	30.6	28.8
Audio - Visual	20.9	30.1

Teaching methods as mentioned above are useful for explaining the subject contents to the students. The NIOS gives importance to audio-visual method in teaching and it supplies cassetes on different topics to the study centres. But it is evident that audio-visual equipments are not very frequently used in PCP. The response of the students also corroborates this fact. A large number of students in both the States agreed that maps, charts and globes are used in PCP classes. However, the PCP classes are not adequate for comprehension of all the subject matters and the NIOS students differ among themselves in the level of comprehension.

Table 6 : Arrangement made by students to sort out their study problems

Arrangements	Bihar	Jharkhand
Additional time at centre	29.0	-
Facility for self reading at centre	16.0	6.0
Discussion with friends	32.0	26.0
Help of guardians	10.0	8.0
Private tuition	13.0	11.0
Do nothing	-	49.0

It is evident that some centres made additional arrangement for some students. In some, facility of space for self reading is provided. However, in many cases, friends help the NIOS students. In Jharkhand about 50% students do not do any thing even when they find difficulty in understanding the subject matter.

At the same time teachers of both the States feel that after attaining PCP classes, the students develop the reading skills as well as the level of comprehension. They claim that they evaluate subject wise learning outcome of the students by different techniques.

Table 7 : Difficulties in running Accredited Institutions

Items	Bihar	Jharkhand	Total
Insufficient No. of prospectus supplied	14.0	42.0	27.0
Supply of prospectus in wrong language	-	33.0	15.0
Late supply of study materials	43.0	33.0	38.0
Inadequate information flow from NIOS	14.0	25.0	19.0
Lack of proper advertisement for admission	50.0	42.0	46.0
Supply of study materials in wrong medium	21.0	25.0	23.0
Inadequate financial support	36.0	67.0	42.0

The most obvious difficulty in running an Accredited Institution is the lack of proper advertisement regarding admission and other related matters. Inadequate financial support, late supply of study materials, supply of insufficient number of prospectus and supply of study materials in wrong medium stand in the way of the proper functioning of these centres and the NIOS system as such.

A probe into the issue of inadequate financial support reveals that staff is not satisfied with the amount of honorarium paid to them. Irregular payment of honorarium further escalates dissatisfaction among them.

Table 8 : Suggestions for improvement in NIOS system

Suggestions	Bihar		Jharkhand	
	Co-ordinator	Teacher	Co-ordinator	Teacher
Facilitation /Monitoring	100.0	100.0	100.0	100.0
Timely supply of study materials	50.0	45.0	50.0	55.0
Enrichment of library	21.0	10.0	17.0	18.0
Raising number of PCP classes	43.0	16.0	42.0	16.0
Audio-visual kits on all subjects	14.0	13.0	17.0	11.0
Increase in financial package	57.0	30.0	50.0	40.0
Widely advertisement regarding NIOS system	50.0	-	42.0	-

The most important suggestion given by the Co-ordinators and the teachers is that there should be regular facilitation or monitoring and supervision. It was reported that in the earlier years, facilitation was used to be done in some centres. Half of the Co-ordinators of both the States did not ever meet any Facilitators in their centres.

Another important suggestion refers to the timely supply of study materials. Half of the Co-ordinators and the teachers suggest this. More number of Co-ordinators than the teachers suggest for the increase in the number of PCP classes on each subject. However, they have not suggested the ideal number of PCP per subject.

Suggestion for advertisement in T.V., radio and in local newspapers regarding NIOS courses, admission and other related matters has been given by nearly half of the Co-ordinators. They think that this is the first and foremost step in making NIOS system popular in the countryside.

(b) Accredited Vocational Institutions (AVI)

Table 9: Vocational courses followed by the students

Courses	Bihar	Jharkhand	Total
Certificate in Computer Applications	52.0	-	26.0
Beauty Culture	4.0	-	2.0
Cutting & Tailoring	11.0	38.0	25.0
Refrigeration & Air Conditioning	9.0	6.0	8.0
Radio & T.V. Technician	10.0	4.0	7.0
Radiography	5.0	-	2.0
Solar Energy Technician	8.0	11.0	9.0
Paramedical Courses	-	10.0	5.0
Electrical Technician	-	30.0	15.0

Course on computer application has a great demand in Bihar. But in Jharkhand, a large number of students opt for cutting and tailoring and electrical trade. The students who have been doing computer application course have suggested for modification and updating of its syllabus, otherwise the job potentiality of the passed out students will be bleak.

Table 10 : Sources of information regarding AVI courses

Sources	Bihar	Jharkhand	Total
Newspaper	29.0	18.0	24.0
Academic centres	36.0	59.0	48.0
Friends	17.0	16.0	17.0
Guardians	10.0	07.0	08.0
NIOS Regional Office	03.0	-	01.0
Others	05.0	-	02.0

It is clear that AVI acts as a major source of information regarding the courses. Information from Newspaper was obtained by nearly one fourth of the students. Friends and guardians also play important role in disseminating information.

The majority of the Co-ordinators of both the States say that adequate advertisement about the courses and other related topics is not made by the NIOS. So the views of the Co-ordinators corroborate with the response of the students.

Table 11 : Availability of facilities at AVI

Suggestions	Bihar		Jharkhand	
	Co-ordinator	Student	Co-ordinator	Student
Space for Class-room	94.0	100.0	98.0	100.0
Space for practical classes	94.0	100.0	98.0	100.0
Library	30.0	88.0	45.0	80.0
Furniture	100.0	100.0	100.0	100.0
Electricity	100.0	100.0	100.0	100.0
Drinking water	100.0	100.0	100.0	100.0
Toilet	100.0	100.0	100.0	100.0
Play ground	40.0	88.0	34.0	100.0
Audio-visual equipment	46.0	75.0	49.0	80.0
Black-board	100.0	100.0	100.0	100.0

It is evident that some students from both the States are not satisfied with the space available for class rooms and practical classes. Library facilities do not exist in some AVIs. Non-availability of audio-visual equipments have also been reported by some students and the Co-ordinators. Thus it is clear that proper academic facilities are not available in some AVIs.

Table 12 : Difficulties concerning AVI under NIOS

Difficulties	Bihar	Jharkhand
Supply of insufficient number of prospectus	50.0	60.0
Late supply of study materials	62.0	60.0
Inadequate financial support	50.0	50.0
Non-payment to teachers and Coordinators	62.0	60.0
No timely action by NIOS on Coordinator's report	25.0	—
NIOS certificate not recognized for employment	25.0	40.0

Although the responses of the Co-ordinators vary, it is quite clear that these difficulties reduce the popularity of vocational education, sponsored by NIOS. Some Coordinators have reported that non-acceptance of NIOS certificate for employment, non-payment of honorarium in time to teachers and Co-ordinators has non-motivating effect on the study centres. Thus due to these factors the AVIs face difficulty to secure higher enrolment of students and in running the centres.

Table 13 : Suggestions for improvement of AVIs and NIOS system

Suggestions	Bihar	Jharkhand
Timely supply of study materials	60.0	85.0
Timely payment of honorarium	74.0	69.0
Proper advertisement about NIOS	60.0	85.0
Proper supervision and monitoring	51.0	38.0
Raising the number of PCP sessions	38.0	-
Visit of Fcilitator	57.0	23.0
Supply of audio-visual kits	34.0	61.0
Recognition of NIOS certificate	-	38.0

Suggestions given by the teachers and the Co-ordinators reflect inherent constraints of NIOS. Study material which is a basic pre-requisite for an enrolled student does not always reach on time at the study centre. Similarly regular PCP session and visit of Facilitators can increase the potential of the students, but this never happens. Lack of proper supervision and monitoring is also a matter of grave concern for the overall improvement of AVIs. In Jharkhand Coordinators raised the issue of non-recognition of NIOS certificate. According to them non-recognition of NIOS certificate will lead to poor enrolment at NIOS study centres. Frustration among teachers and Co-ordinators due to delay of honorarium payment is clear in both the States and it also works as a hurdle in the growth of NIOS system.

(c) Special Accredited Institutions for Education of the Disadvantaged (SAIED)

Table 14 : Suggestions for improvement in NIOS system

Facility	Bihar		Jharkhand	
	Co-ord-inator	Teacher	Co-ord-inator	Teacher
Class-room	100.0	100.0	100.0	100.0
Furniture	100.0	100.0	77.0	100.0
Drinking water	100.0	100.0	67.0	100.0
Toilet	100.0	100.0	100.0	100.0
Playground	100.0	100.0	67.0	67.0
Electricity	100.0	100.0	100.0	100.0
Audio-visual equipments	43.0	100.0	100.0	100.0
Library	100.0	100.0	72.0	100.0
Laboratory/Workshop	100.0	100.0	20.0	33.0

It is evident that there is difference in the response between the students and the Coordinators in Jharkhand and Bihar with regard to availability of different facilities. Bulk of students in Bihar do not agree with the Coordinators that the study centres have audio-visual equipmnets. However, on the whole, it can be said that the SAIEDs have the facilities for organizing the different courses of study.

Table 15 : Suggestions for strengthening NIOS programme

Suggestions	Co-ordinator	Teacher
Timely supply of study materials	40.0	70.0
Supply of audio-visual kits	40.0	59.0
Regular visit of Facilitator	60.0	35.0
Increase in number of PCP classes	40.0	35.0
Raising honorarium amount	60.0	53.0
Enrichment of library	20.0	18.0
Thorough campaign of NIOS	80.0	88.0

Suggestions given by the teachers and the Coordinators point to the fact that proper campaign about NIOS need to be made throughout the countryside. This is particularly necessary for attracting the disadvantaged groups of people in the NIOS system. Availability of audio-visual kits on different subjects and regular visits of Facilitators will be a boon for proper functioning of Open schools. Timely release of honorarium and raising its rate will be an added impetus to organize Open schools in SAIEDs.

The Facilitators are the academician serving or retired, or educational administrators of the area who provide their expertise for the benefit of the staff of the study centre and the students enrolled with them. For quality control an academic Facilitator is given the responsibility of one study centre. He is required to pay 10 to 12 visits during an academic year to the centre and oversee the services provided by the administration and the teachers.

Overview

Although advertisement in Newspapers regarding Open schooling is published, it is not an important source of information to the students or their guardians. More than two thirds of the students interviewed in the study learnt about it from their friends and the study centres. It appears that the people living in remote areas are hardly aware of Open schooling.

Institutions have the necessary infrastructural facilities to perform the functions of study centres. But enrolment of students in the institutions is quite low. Some centres have very few students on their rolls.

It is suggested by some centre Coordinators that making provision for admission throughout the year is likely to encourage higher enrolment as the students from rural areas can enroll themselves at their own convenience.

About three-fourths of the students in the Open schools belongs to the upper and backward castes. One of the five students are from the scheduled tribe and one out of twenty students is from scheduled caste.

Parents of the bulk of the students enrolled in AIs and AVIs are in service and business. But the majority of the SAIED students are from the family of cultivators and agricultural labourers. However, on the whole it is the socially and economically advantaged sections of the population that have been deriving benefit from Open schooling.

Easy admission procedure, flexibility in passing the course, less expensive education, availability of study materials and provision of Personal Contact Programme seem to be the major factors for enrolment in Open schooling.

The majority of the students in AIs and AVIs have been pursuing their study in English. This implies that they are neither from poor families nor school drop-outs. They seem to be at least second generation learners.

It is observed that the majority of the students who did not qualify for admission in good formal schools, have joined Open schools. Some schools which have study centres, have advised their own students to join Open schools and attend classes with regular students, of course on payment of regular fees.

Their observation seem to be tenable if the motivational factors for admission in Open schools, accepting English as a medium of learning and occupational background of the parents are taken together. However, the NIOS system seems to be a boon for those students who can not withstand the competition for admission in good formal schools.

Timely supply of study materials to the study centres is not always made. It causes inconvenience to the students. Sometimes the study materials contain mistakes in language of the content.

Study materials are read by most of the students. The majority of the students who comprehend the subjects without the help of others, find the study materials simple, clear and fascinating.

One third of the students who find the study materials difficult on account of complex language, subject matter and difficult exercises, seek help of friends, guardians and teachers for better comprehension.

The number of Personal Contact Programme classes on a subject is decided by the number of students enrolled in it. Fewer the students, fewer is the number of PCP. In a number of study centres only a few students are on their rolls. Thus the PCP classes allotted to them are inadequate to cover all the subjects.

According to NIOS norms, PCP classes are to be held on Saturdays and Sundays. But this is not always followed. These are conducted mainly on holidays.

Routine of PCP classes is put on notice boards of the study centres. Majority of students get prior information about it. Timing of PCP classes also suits the students.

Teachers admit that attendance in PCP classes on academic subjects is poor. It is observed that in the institutions having small number of students, PCP classes are not generally conducted.

The NIOS is expected to provide audio-visual cassettes on different subjects to the study centres. These are not supplied to all the study centres. The use of cassettes in PCP classes is rare. Many institutions do not have T.V., V.C.P. and other equipments for the purpose.

Library facility is available in the study centres. But the students are not allowed to borrow books from there. Only a few of them avail reading facility.

Facilitation is an important aspect of NIOS system. But during 2001-2002, no Facilitator was appointed. Contrary to this some former Facilitators were of the view that the study centres also do not extend necessary cooperation in Facilitation work.

However, the National Institution of Open schooling seeks to reach out to the unreached sections of the society such as school drop-outs, out of school children in villages and towns, girls and womens, handicapped persons and ex-servicemen. It opens an avenue for continuing education to those who have missed the opportunity to complete schooling and prepares them to stand on their own legs.

But the role of teachers in the Open school system is very different from that in the formal system. At present it is the formal school teachers who are functioning in the PCP. The mind set and orientation of the teachers in these two streams is not the same. They need special skills to intensively interact with the Open school students. The time at their disposal is very small compared to that in the formal system. They require to built strong rapport so that whatever they teach is comprehended by the students. For this, it is necessary to make an all out effort at capacity building for the new assignment. It is necessary to change their orientation through systematic training. This is all the more necessary as unwilling teachers can not motivate students to make a success of their efforts.

Bulk of students at NIOS are not drawn from the disadvantaged sections of the community. This calls for special drive on the part of the administration to attract the disadvantaged sections of the community for which this scheme has been devised. Awareness about the NIOS system should be promoted through the Panchayati Raj Institution and other departments of the administration which are operational in the villages as well in towns. As a matter of fact, the best disseminators of NIOS system could be those who have passed out of the system.

Orientation courses should be also arranged from time to time for the Coordinators and Facilitators, as they have important roles to play in the entire NIOS scheme. These orientation courses will make them aware about the latest development in the field of Open schooling and to adopt the methods to make the programme more successful . At the same time the

Facilitator should be more closely connected with the programme. If they are given powers, they should also be held accountable to the administration.

Last, but not the least, for setting of a study centre, there should be a minimum level of viability. The number of students enrolled determines the enrolments of teachers as well as the number of Personal Contact Programme (PCP) classes in each subject. It is not a hidden fact that at many places the enrolment is so poor that the number of PCP classes was hardly sufficient to meet the needs of the students. Such a situation would frustrate the entire objectives of the NIOS system and therefore requires immediate attention.

References

Department of Education (1992) : Education For All, The Indian Scene : Widening Horizons, Ministry of Human Resource Development, Govt of India, New Delhi.

Mehrotra, C. M., C. David Hollister and Lawenence Megahay (2001) : Distance Learning : Principles For Effective Design, Delivery and Evaluation, Crowin Press, Inc., London.

Ramaiah, Y. R. (1998) : Distance Education And Open Learning, Mittal Publications, New Delhi.

Sachchidananda (2002) : Role of Academic Facilitation At Study Centres of National Open School in Bihar And Jharkhand, Sulabh Institute of Development Studies, Patna.

Sharma, K. D. and D. V. Sharma (2002) : Open Learning System In India, Allied Publishers, New Delhi.

Williams, Paprock and Covington (1998) : Distance Learning: The Essential Guide, Sage Publications, London.

World Bank (1997) : Primary Education In India, Allied Publishers, New Delhi.

6

COMMUNITY PARTICIPATION IN PRIMARY EDUCATION : The Uttar Pradesh Experience

RAJ KUMAR PANDEY

This study of community participation through Village Education Committee in primary education in Uttar Pradesh covers the two blocks each from Gorakhpur and Varanasi. The main focus is on the activities and effectiveness of Village Education Committees (VEC) in involving the local community in school education. It brings out why people's participation is not forthcoming to the degree desired.

The Kothari Commission was set up in 1964 to study the whole scenario of education including the role of local bodies in education. The Education Commission observed that "The close involvement of schools with their communities is a principle of great educational significance and this is the direction in which we should move." Community involvement in the management of school and associated matters, the VEC which has been conceived in National Policy on Education (NPE) and Plan of Action (POA) as a delivery system for the programmes of mass education particularly elementary education and an institutional framework at grassroot level, needs to be made more effective, with community participation.

Thus under the 73rd Amendment, Panchayats have been formed for a village or a group of villages. The Panchayat has elected representatives. Besides this each Panchayat may constitute a Village Education Committee (VEC) which would be responsible for administration of the delegated programmes in the field of education at the village level. The major responsibility of the VECs should be operationalization of micro level planning and school mapping in the village through systematic house to house survey and periodic discussions with the parents. It should be the endeavour of the committee that every child in every family participate in the primary education. In these activities they will be provided expert guidance and support from DIET. The state government may consider entrusting the following functions to the VEC :

1. Generation and sustenance of awareness among the village community ensuring participation of all segments of population.
2. Developing teacher and community partnership to oversee and manage the effective and regular functioning of the schools.

Meaning of community participation

Participation is defined as a voluntary contribution by the people in one or another of the public programmes supposed to contribute to national development but the people are not expected to take part in shaping the programme or in criticizing its contents.

Participation includes people's involvement in decision - making processes, in implementing programmes, their sharing in benefits of development programmes, and their involvement in efforts to evaluate such programmes (Cohen and Uphoff, 1977). In this regard participation is viewed as an active process in which the participants take initiatives and actions that are stimulated by their own thinking and by deliberations over which they exert effective control. The idea of passive participation which only involves the people in actions that have been thought out or designed by others and controlled by others is unacceptable (ACC Task Force and Working Group on Rural Development Programme Harmonisation, Rome 1978). People's participation is essentially to do with economic and political relationships within the wider society ; it is not just a matter of involvement in project activities but rather the process by which rural people are able to organise themselves and, through their own organization, are able to identify their own needs, share in design, implement, and evaluate participatory action (FAO, 1982).

Community Participation is an active process by which beneficiary or client groups influence the direction and execution of a development project with a view to enhancing their well-being in terms of income, personal growth, self reliance, or other values they cherish (Paul, 1987).

For involving the community in development, particularly educational development, it will be necessary to understand the concept of community and participation, and make an assessment of needs and resources, within the frame work of socio-cultural, ethnic and economic dynamics.

A community is generally defined as a group of people who have common interest and work together. A community is a unit of social organization, which can potentially meet a person's physiological, psychological and social needs. Communities differ greatly from one another e.g. rural, urban, tribal etc.

Community participation is a process of activities comprising people's involvement in decision making, contributing to the development efforts, sharing equitably the benefits derived there from.

Community participation can be of three types. Participation is sometimes attempted through force or coercion. This runs counter to the basic principles of our democratic polity. Such participation can not be sustained for long. The second type includes attempt to secure participation through issuance of government orders, which again is ineffective for the realization of main objective of active involvement of the people. The third type is spontaneous participation where people organize themselves on voluntary basis and initiate action. In most of the cases. However, the deprived sections will have to be made aware of benefits accruing from development and their capacity to act collectively through sustained efforts of a change agency. Thus, it becomes an essential task of voluntary organizations, action groups and administration committed to the task of genuine development to induce and sustain participation of the people in the development programmes. In the context of education, the aim should be democratic involvement of the people in contributing to the educational development, share equitably the benefits there from and participate in the planning and management of various formal and non-formal educational programmes.

In the Indian context the importance of community participation in development has been recognized right from the first Five year plan. It called for making, adequate arrangements for enlisting public co-operation and association from the very beginning.

The essential need is to involve people in the process of development. The attitude of passive observance and total dependence on the government for developmental activities has become all pervasive. It has to be altered to a pro-active attitude of people taking initiative themselves. In the process of development, people must operate and the government must co-operate.

In the Eighth plan, for the first time a new direction was being given to achieve these objectives by the adoption of institutional approach. The Planning Commission has now worked out institutional strategies which will mean creating or strengthening various people's institutions at the district, block and village level in order to synthesize the purposes of investment envisaged in the central plan with optimization of benefits at the grassroots level by relating these programmes to the needs of people. Panchayats and Nagar Palikas, elected by the people, will have to play a large role in formulating and implementing the developmental projects in their areas. They should be vested with adequate financial resources, technical / managerial inputs and decision making authority. Involvement of voluntary agencies and other people's institutions is essential for effective micro level participatory planning.

An overhaul of the system of planning and management of education has received high priority. Among other things, decentralization and the creation of a spirit of autonomy for educational institutions giving pre-eminence to peoples involvement. The association of non-governmental agencies and voluntary effort, and inducting more women in the planning and management of education have been stressed.

Community Participation and Village Education Committee

The National Policy on Education and Plan of Action have emphasized the importance of decentralizing planning and management of education at all levels and involving people in the process. Decentralization implies democratic participation by elected representatives of people in decision making at the district, sub-division and panchayat levels. It also ensures democratic participation of elected representatives of people in decision making and to mobilize the community there upon. Thus for the purpose of involving the community in development, particularly educational development, it will be necessary to understand the concept of community participation and make an assessment of needs and resources within the framework of socio-cultrual, ethnic and economic dynamics.

From development point of view, the purpose of

education must be to rationalize attitudes as well as to impart knowledge and skills. In India, education has largely been stagnant for a long time and where attitudes antagonistic to development have taken firm root and has become institutionalized, the changing of attitudes requires far greater emphasis as far as human resource development is concerned. The required participation in elementary education has to come from social strata and region which are more difficult to reach and therefore the goal of Universalization of elementary education still remains elusive. Denying people access to elementary education not only means a denial of mobility so vital for survival; it also reflects a degree of social injustice that is intolerable. There is a growing expectation that governance will improve following the 73rd and 74th constitutional amendments and establishment or formal participatory institutions like Village Education Committee. This can happen only if efforts are made to simultaneously Universalize elementary education. After all, the quality of decisions, the ability of the community to participate actively in decision making, and to demand transparency and public accountability will be contingent upon how people understand and act, and ultimately upon the levels of education attainment.

With the enactment of the 73rd and 74th Amendment (Panchayati Raj Act) 1992, the focus is now on democratically elected bodies at the district, subdivision, Panchayat and municipal level. Each Panchayat would constitute a Village Education Committee (VEC) which could be responsible for the administration of education programmes at the village level. Ensuring participation in primary education of every child in every family would be one of the prime aims of VECs.

Village Education Committee (VEC) in Uttar Pradesh

For Uttar Pradesh the concept of community involvement in management of education is not new. In the colonial period also most of the religious institutions meant for imparting education at the primary level were looked after by the community. Gradually after independence things changed and management of primary education become a State affair, but even though, somehow or the other community involvement was never ignored. The Constitution of VEC as made by the Government order. Before that VEC was in existence in many of the villages but not in the present form. Now it is mandatory for every school to function under a VEC. In other words the school can not run without a VEC as most of the authority is vested with the VEC, like handling of the bank account, routine supervision of the school, apart from conducting micro-planning. In the State, constitution of the VEC is the responsibility of the Gram Panchayat and the structure is as below :

President	-	Gram Pradhan
Member Secretary	-	Headmaster
Members	-	

1. Deputy Pradhan of the Gram Panchayat
2. Elected Female member of the Gram Panchayat
3. Elected Scheduled Caste member of Gram Panchayat
4. Elected Scheduled Tribe member of Gram Panchayat (if any)
5. Elected member of Gram Panchayat (other than SC/ST members)
6. Three Supervisor of Basic Schools (nominated by ABSA)
7. Member from Nehru Yuva Kendra /NGO/Mahila Mandal/Mahila Samakhya (nominated by Pradhan for one year)
8. Guardian of any handicap student (Nominated by Pradhan)

All sorts of consultancy and training are provided to

the VEC by DIET and Block Resource Centre (BRC). There is a proper networking from the office of District Magistrate to CRC and vice versa. In every month the VEC organizes a meeting generally at the school campus where issues are discussed. The outcome of the meeting is maintained in a register.

Profile of VEC Members of VECs

Profile of members are discussed below through tables.

Table 1 : Gender-wise distribution of VEC Members

Gender	(N=240)
Male	65.40%
Female	34.58%

Most of the members of VEC were male.

Table 2 : Caste categories

Caste	Percentage
General	15.8
SC	41.6
OBC	39.5
Minorities	2.9
Total	100.0

Most of members of VEC belong to SC while high percentage of members belong to OBC. This shows that representation of all castes in VEC.

Table 3 : Occupation of VEC members

Occupation	N=240
Farming	54.1
Business	13.5
Service	5.4
Others (Labour, domestic work)	27.0
Total	100.0

Majority of the members of VEC were in the farming category.

Table 4 : Educational profile

Education	U.P.
Illiterate	15.0
Non-matric	55.83
Matric	15.0
Inter	7.08
Graduate	6.25
Post Graduate	0.83

Above table reveals that about majority of the respondents were non-matric.

Role of VECs in promoting community mobilization and participation

Community participation and empowerment in primary education has been discussed through the performance and role of VECs in the table mentioned below :

Table 5 : VEC activities

Sl No.	Activities	Percentage
1.	Construction of Class room	64.16
2.	Fixing handpump	46.66
3.	White washing of class rooms	3.75
4.	Construction of toilet	43.33
5.	Construction of boundary	6.25
6.	Plantation	5.41
7.	Increased enrolment	39.58

Respondents gave multiple answers about the activities of VEC. Construction of classrooms, fixing up handpumps and construction of toilets were the some important activities of VEC members. Raising enrolment levels was the next important priority.

Table 6 : Activities of the VEC members in the eyes of opinion leaders (N=240)

Sl No.	Activities	Percentage
1.	Regular supervision of schools	63.33
2.	Consult school teachers regarding problems	8.33
3.	Regular maintenance of building	35.00
4.	No contribution	8.33

Most of the opinion leaders were of the view that the VEC members regularly supervise schools. A lower percentage of respondents said that the VEC members looked after school maintenance. But one section of the community totally disagree with this view. In their opinion the VEC members especially the Pradhan visit school premises only to claim commission from contractors. There are very few active VEC members who listen to grievances of the teachers. In case of female Pradhan this supervision of construction work is performed by proxy. This situation cannot change unless the VEC members realize their full responsibility. For this a proper work oriented training is essential. Not less important is the role of local villagers. They must also come forward and restrain the VEC members from misutilizing developmental funds.

Table 7: Efforts made by the VEC to enhance people's participation

Sl No.	Activities	N=240
1.	Made villagers aware of education	65.83
2.	Consultation held at the meeting of Gram Sabha	5.83
3.	Made door to door canvassing	21.25
4.	Any other	6.66

A large number of respondents reported that VEC members made the villagers aware of education. They made door to door canvassing for extension of education. VEC has worked for the retention for the students. Virtually it has increased the retention in the school.

Table 8: Role of villagers in solving educational problems according to VEC members

N=240

Sex & caste	Yes(%)	No(%)	Total (%)
Female			
General	28.57	71.42	16.86
OBC	39.28	60.71	33.73
SC	7.69	92.30	46.98
Minorities	50.0	50.0	2.40
Total	22.89	77.10	34.58
Male			
General	4.16	95.83	15.28
OBC	20.89	79.10	42.67
SC	11.47	88.52	38.85
Minorities	40.0	60.0	3.18
Total	15.28	84.71	65.41
Grand Total	17.91	82.08	100.0

This table reveals opinion of the VEC members regarding people's participation in solving education related problems. 17.91% VEC members were of the opinion that people participate in solving educational problem. In the female category about 22.89% respondents were of this view where as in the male category the response was 15.28%. In both the categories, the VEC members from the minority community were more affirmative about people's participation. The greatest challenge facing the country today as it strives to reach the goals of 'Education for All' lies in changing people's perceptions. But still mobilizing and empowering the broadest possible range of personnel at the grassroot level will not be enough. People's representatives as well as educational functionaries need to be prepared to cope with the transition and to discharge their responsibilities. On a practical plane, the education system, the state and the society as a whole need to internalize a broader functional view of education, a view which recognizes and defines education as a dynamic, cumulative lifelong process encompassing a wide ranging diversity of learning opportunities applying to all children, particularly those belonging to disadvantaged groups. The combination of political will and popular support can form powerful, virtually irresitable instruments of change and progress. It is this ethos of coordinated, participative working that needs to be extended. While the State Governments have their full share of responsibilities, in the final analysis, it is people's involvement in educational reconstruction which will make the crucial difference.

About 76% teachers were of the view that the VEC works as a link between teachers and guardians. It was often noticed that the VEC members were used by the teachers to convince guardians regarding the shortcomings of the school. If guardians complain to the teachers about shortage of seating mat or non-functional toilet then in certain cases mostly the VEC members are asked to intervene. On the whole it can be concluded that the VEC members are used by the teachers mostly to shed their responsibility instead of encouraging the guardians to send their children to school regularly.

Parents are now more concerned about their children's education than they were twenty years back. Recent changes in parental attitudes towards female education are particularly encouraging. Parental motivation is likely to continue to rise in future, perhaps more rapidly through public intervention if this trend can be accelerated.

The interaction between the guardians and the VEC members is yet not up to the desired extent as far as regular interactions are concerned. One of the reasons is the large presence of women in the education committee. The 'purda' system and their unwillingness to come out of the cocoon is a big hurdle.

The nature of guardian - teacher relation varies a great deal between different villages. Perhaps the most common pattern is one of scant interaction between guardians and teachers. But in all the circumstances, the potential tool for generating guardian - teacher cooperation, the Village Education Committee has failed to perform its duty. Villagers are aware of the poor performance of VEC, but no one is ready to explore them.

The reason behind one of the objectives of VEC in motivating the community in opening and construction of new schools is the fact that in every village there is some land in the possession of Gram Sabha and they have the authority to use it. If the members of the Gram Sabha find that there is some land in the possession of Gram Sabha and they have the authority to use it, in case there is need for a school in their village, they can allocate some land for construction of school. In construction work also they can take financial support from the villagers. In some villages, the Gram Sabha has provided land and in some villages construction work has been done by the villagers when they thought that there is no alternative left and the children of the village are not getting education due to shortage of classrooms. Good relationship exists between VEC and Gram Sabha. Through that efforts the enrolment rate has gone up and children are being sent to the school regularly by guardians. The achievements of the VEC can be seen through the following table:

Table 9: Achievements of the VEC in the eyes of Opinion leaders

N=120

Response	Percentage
Construction of school building	61.67
Repair of school building	4.17
Construction of bathroom	40.83
Construction of boundary wall	11.67
Fixing of hand pump	37.50
Plantation	5.83
Raising enrolment	33.33

Most of the opinion leaders were of the view that the VEC has constructed school building. A lesser percentage believed that bathrooms were constructed by the VEC. The VEC was credited with increase in enrolment rate by one third respondents. Some respondents were of the opinion that the VEC had helped lower dropout rate and upgraded villagers' awareness about education.

Table 10: Initiatives taken by VEC members to attract deprived sections to school

N=120

Activities	**Percentage**
Guardians have been encouraged	62.91
Made aware about scholarship	31.25
Free books provided	0.83
Mid day meals distributed	12.50

The bulk of VEC members held that guardians have been encouraged to send their children to the schools. Some respondents informed that the guardians about the scholarship scheme to motivate them to send their children to the schools. A small percentage believed that midday meal was a big motivation.

Despite these incentives Musahars and Muslims are indifferent to education. Their experience of the educated in their own community is painful. No efforts were being made to win the confidence of these people either by the school or by the VEC, this is a matter of grave concern. Their only excuse is that poverty restrains them from going to school.

Table 11: Micro planning exercise

N = 240

Activities	**(Percentage)**
Fixing handpumps	56.25
Construction of classroom	74.16
Construction of toilet	56.66
Construction of boundary wall	13.75

Respondents highlighted multiple answers regarding micro-planning exercise. Nearly half of the respondent felt that handpumps were fixed to ease the drinking water problem. A large percentage of respondents held that classrooms were built for the overall development of schools. Some of the respondents reported repair and white washing of school building and other works like plantation.

The ground level reality is different. VEC members are not enough capable or trained to conduct micro planning. Such planning is done by the school teachers who procure the signature of the VEC members. Therefore on the whole in both the districts, the requirements of micro planning are met by teachers not by VEC or the community members.

More or less, in every school the enrolment rate has gone up. But still some sections of the community are reluctant to participate. Mostly VEC members show no interest in the educational work. The Pradhan who is head of both the institutions (Gram Sabha and VEC) devotes more time to the Gram Sabha and shows less interest in the educational development work.

Reasons for poor participation

The reasons behind low participation by the community in primary education are lack of educated members, lack of training and dearth of knowledgeable members of VECs. VEC is the Committee for promoting more people's participation in education but there is lack of management information system (MIS) to monitor and coordinate VECs.

The management and functioning of the schools should be more than a local concern than a departmental function regulated through bureaucratic channels. There should be social mobilization programme for increasing community participation but unfortunately it is not forthcoming.

Problems in active participation of VECs in education are discussed through the table below :

Table 12: Problems of Village Education Committee

Problems	Percentage
Lack of funds	35.41
Members ineffective	21.66
Members demand honorarium for their work	16.25
Lack of official supervision	16.25
Female members not active	10.00
Meetings irregular	9.58
Lack of knowledge among the members about their functions	9.58
Want of time among the members	7.91
Lack of educated members	7.91

Respondents pointed out multiple problems of VEC. The main problem is lack of fund to perform its function. Funds available are not adequate and due to this they are unable to create a education friendly environment in the village. Some of the respondents reported that some members rarely attend the meetings. Some of the VEC members were of the view that the work performed by the committee should come under regular supervision by some independent agency. They believe that the fear of supervision may compel the members to actively discharge their duty failing which provisions for replacement may be made. Some of the respondents were of the view that there was lack of coordination between VEC members and headmaster. Even all members of VEC are not given equal weightage.

Table 13 : Problems of VEC in the eyes of guardians

N=120

Response	Percentage
VEC members are illiterate	64.17
Members are ineffective	27.50
Lack of financial assistance to members	12.50
VEC members lack time	5.00
Women VEC member do not have time	9.17
Lack of villager's participation	0.83
Lack of fund in the Committee	6.67

Guardians highlighted multiple problems of VEC. Majority of the respondents were of the opinion that the VEC members are themselves illiterate and thus they are not competent to solve problems concerning education. This is more or less supported by the view of respondents that VEC members lack adequate knowledge about their functions. Women VEC members are also reluctant to discharge their duties according to 9.17% respondents. Meetings were not held regularly. Lack of resources was a grave problem.

Table 14: Main problems of VEC according to Opinion leaders

N=120

Response	**Percentage**
Members are illiterate	48.33
Poor attendance at meeting	15.00
Lack of coordination among members	12.50
Women members less cooperative	11.67
Lack of co-ordination from teachers	5.83
Members are unaware of their duties	10.00
Meeting hours are not convenient	8.33
Lack of funds	5.00

Opinion leaders pointed out multiple problems of the VEC. Almost half the opinion leaders held that the VEC members are illiterate and therefore , they fail to perform their duty. Attendance at the meetings of VEC is poor according to 15% respondents. Some of the respondents reported that the coordination among the members is also poor. About 15% respondents urged payment of honorarium to VEC members for the time they give. Some respondents attributed lack of awareness among certain sections of the people as a major problem for the VEC. Members of VEC lacked power and resources. There was lack of awareness among some section of people.

Suggestions for the solution of the problems of the VEC

VEC members gave multiple suggestions for the solution of the problems. One third VEC members were

Table 15: Suggestions by the VEC members

N=220

Response	Percentage
Adequate fund to be provided	33.75
Supervision of VEC by authorities	28.33
Honorarium to be given to each member	18.75
Members of VEC to be educated	13.33
Meeting time should be convenient	8.75
Adequate training to be provided to members	9.58

of the opinion that provision for more funds can solve their problems. Supervision of the work performed by the VEC was essential according to one fourth of respondents. 13.33% respondents hold that provision should be made to make only educated villagers eligible for membership of VEC. They suggested that only active women should be made members. There should be provision of punishment to the guilty VEC members. Wheat, scholarship etc. should be equally distributed to students by the VEC members. VEC should be given more powers.

Table 16: Guardian's suggestions to make VEC effective

N=120

Suggestions	Percentage
Literate people should be made member of VEC	65.83
Supervision of VEC	21.67
Provision for financial assistance to the member	9.17
Fund should be provided to the Committee	6.67

The bulk of respondents were of the opinion that the only remedy for making the Committee strong is by making literate person eligible for VEC. Making of provision for supervision of the work performed by the VEC was essential in the view of 21.67% respondents. Provision for more and regular training to the VEC members was supported by some of the respondents. About 3.33% respondents hold the view that the reservation for women should be reduced. They were just holding positions without any effective participation.

Table 17: Suggestions for solving problems of the VEC according to opinion leaders

N=120

Suggestions	Percentage
Members who are dedicated to education should only be selected	41.67
Supervision of VEC	23.33
Members should be literate	18.33
Distribution of work among each member	8.33
Meeting hours should be convenient	5.83
Provision of honorarium to VEC members	12.50
Attendance in meeting should be compulsory	8.33
Distribution of work among each member	8.33
Committee should be provided financial assistance	5.83

Opinion leaders gave multiple suggestions regarding the solution of the problems. They were of the view that only such members should be included in the committee who are dedicated to education. Supervision of the work performed by the VEC is necessary according to 23.33% respondents who feel that regular supervision will compel members to work in coordination. Due to lack of any financial gain in work looks tiresome to the members. As the provision for honorarium is essential, therefore, this view was supported by 12.5% respondents. About 8.33% respondents were of the view that attendance in meeting should be made compulsory and explanation should be asked from the absentee members. Some of the opinion leaders were in favour of vesting VEC members with more power so that they can work more efficiently. They feel that the VEC members do not have enough authority to arrange things. They should be provided more training.

Following steps are suggested to make the Village

Education Committee more effective in achieving its objectives with people's participation.

1. Immediate steps should be taken to clear the large backlog of VEC members who have not received training. Appropriate training facilities should be created at the block level for this purpose.
2. Quality of training of VEC members should be improved in view of the importance of task expected from them, e.g. supervising primary schools, NFE centres, planning, managing and implementing other educational programme in the village.
3. Suitable mechanism should be developed to actively involve the VEC members and the community in educational activities in the village.
4. The VEC must prepare its quarterly plan of action and implement it accordingly.
5. It must be ensured that all the VECs hold their monthly meeting regularly and keep proper record of the proceedings. Care should be taken to improve attendance of VEC members, critical review of its performance and plan for next month and quality of discussion held in the meeting.
6. Immediate and appropriate follow up activities should be initiated to translate decisions of the meeting into action.
7. Appropriate mechanism should be developed to punish defaulter VEC members. For this a proper routine supervision of financial and physical work performed by the VEC is essential.
8. The practice of proxy participation must be stopped. The prevalence of this practice is the biggest hurdle in generating actual education friendly environment. Defaulting members must be replaced.
9. In this age of science and technology, the

electronic and print media must be exploited to launch a campaign for education inputs to target the deprived sections, especially the girl children by the VEC. In a traditional society, folklore like myths, legends, folktales, folk-songs, proverbs, riddles etc must be exploited in the campaign for education for all.

10. Most of the ground level difficulties pertaining to providing time for bank account operation, participation in meeting and other related activities rest on the issue of compensating for the financial loss of the members. Therefore, there is need to evolve certain rules and regulations for honorarium, T.A. D.A. to the members.
11. The VEC should get full cooperation of the District Education Office, as and when required, to carry out its activitis.
12. The VEC should establish and strengthen inter-sectoral linkages with primary schools, NFE, ICDS, TLC, NGOs and development programmes in the village.
13. The Panchayat leaders should know their actual powers, roles and functions so that the communication gap between them and the officials can be bridged. Therefore, the State government should provide adequate political support to these bodies. Once the grassroot level leaders are empowered the expansion of school education will be smooth.

Overview

The concept of community involvement in management of education is not new. In the colonial period also most of the institutions meant for imparting education at the primary level were looked after by the community. Gradually after independence things changed and management of primary education become a state affair and community involvement was ignored.

The role of community participation and empowerment in primary education in Uttar Pradesh has been assessed through this study. Training provided to the VEC members was neither regular nor of equal duration. It varied from one block to another. This disparity in the training programme affected the efficacy of the VEC members.

Irregularity of meetings and poor participation is a big hurdle in the smooth functioning of the VEC. Generally it has been noticed that the meetings are only organised on paper and the signatures of the members are procured later on.

Securing people's participation from below is not an easy task, as Passmore said "Society as much as nature resist man's plans, it is not wax in the hands of the scientist, the planner, the legislature." In the field of education to increase the acceptability and utilization of resource and make the programme realistic and effective, it is necessary to secure people's participation from all sections of the society. In the absence of proper community support, the micro planning process fails to transfer the management of education to the people through education committee.

The poor and deprived classes often do not show interest in these activities due to lack of awareness. They require regular orientation which is time consuming and expensive. Probably, such problems could be solved by identifying some young community volunteers who could be trained in Participatory Learning and Action (PLA) to became facilitators. There is urgent need to do Action Research for promoting community participation in improving school education in Uttar Pradesh.

Constitution of VEC was according to the constitutional norm. Most of the VEC members were non-matric. This low level of personal education lowers the efficacy of VEC member's participation in the educational development process.

Training provided to the VEC members was neither regular nor of equal duration. It varied from one block to another. This disparity in the training programme affected the efficacy of the VEC members.

Irregularity of meeting and poor participation is a big hurdle in the smooth functioning of the VEC. Generally it has been noticed that the meetings are only organized on paper and the signatures of the members are procured later on. In most of the VEC meetings not more than one third members are present. The rest are engaged in their own agricultural work. Even if a member is free, he does not consider it important to participate in it. The excuse is that meeting hours are not convenient.

Despite many incentives the Musahars and Muslims are averse to education. Their experience of the educated in their community is painful. No efforts are being made to win the confidence of these people by the VEC.

There is need to make the VEC more effective in achieving its objective through providing training and resources to the members of the VECs. Proper monitoring and evaluation should be done regularly. It will provide feed back for the improvement of the functioning of Village Education Committees. Consequently planning and management for school education would be strengthened.

References

Kumar, Niraj (2002) : A Diagnostic Study of Khagaria District (under Sarva Shiksha Abhiyaan), Sulabh Institute of Development Studies, Patna.

Kumar, Somesh (2002) : Methods for Community Participation - A complete Guide for Practitioners, Vistaar Publications, New Delhi.

Lal, Manohar (1995) : Village Education Committee in Ranchi and Sitamarhi, Concurrent Evaluation of Bihar Education Project Council during 1994-95, A. N. Sinha Institute of Social Studies, Patna.

Pandey, Rajkumar (2002) : A Diagnostic Study of Begusarai District (Under Sarva Shiksha Abhiyaan), Sulabh Institute of Development Studies, Patna.

Sachchidananda (2000) : Role of VEC in Community Participation So Far, Sulabh Institute of Development Studies, Patna.

7

PERFORMANCE OF VILLAGE EDUCATION COMMITTEE AND VIDYALAYA SHIKSHA SAMITI IN BIHAR

RAJ KUMAR PANDEY

Background

School system in 19th century Bengal and Bihar, before British influence spread to villages. The teacher was sustained by a combination of fees and contribution in cash and kind from the community. This varied from village to village. Most of the families in the village were not interested in education. Some untouchable castes were denied admission. There was usually no separate, exclusive space for the school, which was often used for other purpose when the school was not functioning. Such education, though more or less totally supported by a section of the community catered to a small population.

In British India, local bodies were set up in the eighties of the 19th century. Apart from other functions, they had the responsibility of organizing school education tool. Zamindars were playing important role in the development of education. The place for school and payment for the teacher was usually given by the Zamindars. There was poor demand for education. Poor people were unable to send their children to schools. Gifts and other things was given to the teacher by children's parents on the eve of festivals.

Changes after independence

Universal Elementary Education became constitutional commitment of independent India. From the late 1960, the government effected a takeover of the administration of schools as well as rural community had no role in school functioning, although managing committees continued in papers. School teachers were low paid. It was felt that education is the responsibility of the government and became a state subject. Education of weaker sections became the concern of the government.

This process led to alienation of the community from education. The idea that everything was the responsibility of the government and not the community. Buildings which were earlier maintained by the local bodies now began to fall into disrepair. The tasks of teacher multiplied. Being government employees, in addition to teaching, teachers had to perform census, election, polio and distribution of mid day meal etc.

Period before 1989 Resolution of the Education Department

Village Education Committee (VECs) were created through the resolution of October 15, 1988 of the Directorate of Primary Education (Bihar). The resolution stated that in the light of the National Education Policy 1986, it was resolved to constitute Village Education Committee / Ward Education Committee aimed at people's participation in ensuring free and compulsory primary education and supervision of the activities of teachers in primary / middle schools, adult education centres, NFE centres and other educational institutions in the rural and urban areas. The VEC was to comprise eleven categories of members. In all, there were fifteen members in a VEC. Mukhiya / Ward Commissioner was to act as ex-officio president and senior most among the Headmasters was to act as member secretary. In addition, there were members from among the guardians, donors, women, SC/ST, minorities, retired government officers having interest in education, social workers, teachers and Headmasters of other schools.

A VEC was created in a revenue village in the rural area and in a ward in the urban area. The District Education Officer and Block Education Officer (DEO, and BEO) along with the Mukhiya of the Panchayat had significant role to play in the constitution of the village education committee. The tenure of the VEC was three years from the date of election of the President. The VEC was to hold a monthly meetings. The Secretary was to write the proceedings, get these approved by the President and send it to the Controlling officer within a week of the meeting. The proceedings book was kept by the Member Secretary. The VEC meeting took place in the school premises. The officers of the Education department may participate in the VEC meeting but without the right to vote. One third of the total members would form quorum for the meeting. The VEC was responsible for ensuring universal access and participation of all children of 6 to 14 years living in the influence zone of the school. It also take care of school building, distribution of books, creation of infrastructural facilities in it.

Emergence of the Bihar Education Project

To bring about a new ferment in the State through educational reconstruction, Bihar Education Project (BEP) has been taken as a joint step of the State Government, Union Government and UNICEF. The objectives of BEP include Universalization of Primary Education (UPE) through formal and non-formal system, drastic reduction in illiteracy particularly in 15-35 age group, provision of equal access to women and the deprived communities for education, relating education to the living and working conditions of the people and laying special emphasis in all educational activities in science and environment and on inculcation of a sense of social justice.

There are some important factors that determine the success of such a programme of educational transformation viz, the formation of Committees at village level and their sustenance throughout, mass mobilization activities for creating a favourable environment quality of training, monitoring system etc.

VEC Under the Bihar Education Project

The Bihar Education Project, since its beginning has undertaken creation of VECs where they did not exist and reconstituting those which were already constituted under the Directorate of Primary Education. The VEC formed under the BEP varied from the VEC under the Primary Education in many respects.

The VEC under the BEP was constituted at the school / village level, through the general meeting of the village and has one third women members. It was not necessary to have panchayat mukhia as the VEC president. New members were selected through general village meetings. Participation of VEC in the construction of school building and distribution of books and other materials was necessary. The members were imparted training to improve their capability.

Initially, the Bihar Education Project adopted the VEC model propagated by the Primary Education Directorate with some modifications like inclusion of member of voluntary agency Anganbari Sevika and Sakhi of Mahila Samakhya. The meeting of VEC was scheduled to be held by weekly. A copy of proceedings of the meeting was to be sent to the district BEP office and the District Education Officer. The headmasters of the concerned schools were made accountable to the VEC. The tenure of the VEC was fixed as three years. The VEC would help the panchayat in conducting village education survey, prepare plans for educational development of the village and implement, monitor and evaluate such plans and mobilise people for participation in these activities. Till March 1993 the VECs were constituted / reconstituted under the BEP on the basis of above model in the BEP districts.

The BEP Council, Patna brought out a comprehensive booklet entitled "Community participation in Primary Education and Village Education Committee" in the year 1994. A new set of guidelines has been incorporated in the booklet, the copies of which were sent to all the VECs in the BEP districts for constitution / reconstitution of VECs.

The new guidelines suggest that the VEC will be constituted at school / village level. The number of VEC members will range from 7 to 15. The members will be selected from the categories of guardians, educationists among the panchayat members, school teachers (Headmaster of local primary / middle school will act as its member secretary) and instructors of adult education and NFE Centres. Where there was no school, the instructor of AE/NFE will act as member-secretary. The members of the VEC will also be drawn from the cooperative society and women. It is compulsory for the Sakhi of the Mahila Samakhya to be the member of the VEC. There will be representative of SC/ST, minorities, Gram Sewak, ANM, Anganbari worker and the village youth.

A person known for his dedication and commitment to the cause of education will be the president of the village education committee. Half of the VEC members will comprise women. The members of the VEC will be selected in Gram Sabha meetings. The members of the VEC will elect a president and a vice-president from amongst them. The Vice-president will chair the VEC meetings in the absence of the president.

The village education committee, as a representative of the village community, has a crucial role to play in the overall development of education. It will prepare education plan, create education friendly environment in the village, and mobilize physical resources. It will see that the resources are properly utilised and there is proper co-ordination between all the development programme in the village. It will initiate a people's movement to spread education among women and educationally deprived sections.

Bihar Education Project has made efforts to facilitate accountability of primary schools and NFE centres to the people through creation of grassroot structure like Village Education Committee (VEC). The findings of the study on Village Education Committee in Sitamarhi concurrent evaluation of Bihar Education Project during 1994-95 are given below.

The BEP Sitamarhi started functioning from January 1992, though it was formally launched on 1st April 1992. In January itself 160 VECs grouped in 16 clusters (of ten revenue villages each) in 16 blocks of the district were constituted. However, on 6th April, 1992 all the 160 VECs were dissolved through an office order of the BEP Sitamarhi. Again on 16th April, 1992 a new circular was issued to reconstitute VECs with village primary school (and not revenue village) as a unit of reconstitution. 1237 primary schools and 309 middle schools in the district were taken up by the BEP around which the VECs were to be constituted. This way 1363 VECs were formed. Since beginning of the BEP a project level subcommittee, comprising the DM, DDC and VEC Component Incharge, was constituted a plan and mange the formation and activities of the VECs in the district. Out of 1363 VECs 640 (i.e. 47%) have been further reconstituted by March, 1994. According to the action plan for 1994-95 the remaining 723 VECs were supposed to be reconstituted by December, 1994.

The VECs have been constituted / reconstituted from time to time on the basis of guidelines prepared by the BEP. They have printed information sheets and hand book in Hindi for VEC members and distributed among the VECs. The contents of the handbook are related to topics like significance and role of VECs, constitution of VECs, activities of VECs, training of VEC members and their responsibilities in the BEP and in the educational upliftment of the village people.

The Reconstitution Team has taken up the task of reorganisation of VECs on the basis of following criteria. The VECs will comprise of 10 to 25 members drawn from among the guardians, teachers, NFE instructor, members of SC/ST and minorities, women (and Sakhi of Mahila Samooh), youth group and persons dedicated to education. One third of the VEC members will come from weaker sections. The persons whose children study in the local school may be eligible to become guardian members. Persons living in the village and having interest in education will also be eligible to become member of the VEC.

Training of VECs

In the reconstituted VECs president and the motivators as well as some VEC members have been imparted training to enable them to perform their job effectively. The VEC president and motivator have been imparted three days residential training. VEC members have been trained through one day non-residential training programme organized by VEC Component Incharge, master trainer and trained VEC presidents and motivators in the respective block areas. The training programme for VEC members have mostly been held in high / middle schools in the respective block areas. Out of 640 reconstituted VECs, training of presidents and motivators was completed in 437 (i.e. 68%) VEC by 31st March, 1994. Similarly more than 1000 VEC members of 121 reconstituted VECs have been trained so far. In four blocks (Dumra, Saidpur, Riga and Sonbarsa) out of 181 reconstituted VECs training of presidents and motivators and members was completed only in 126 VECs.

District Core Team (DCT) Sitarmarhi

The District Core Team has been formed to ensure people's participation in BEP and co-ordinate VECs at the district level. The DCT is broad based. It has a coordinator (Consultant) and eleven members coming form school teachers and office bearers of Village Education Committees.

The DCT identified the problems encountered by the VECs. In the absence of any financial support to the VEC members, the VECs faced difficulty in visiting the district office, making regular correspondence and retaining enthusiasm and interest of the members in the VEC activities. The action on the problems of the school teachers by the concerned authorities has been delayed many times. The DCT encountered problem of proper coordination with VEC at the village level in the absence of any intermediary structure at the block level. Monitoring of progress of VECs was also difficult in the absence of any subsystem between district and village level. However, representatives of different VECs were free to meet the DM, DDC or VEC component incharge in the BEP office at Sitamarhi on every Tuesday to submit progress report and discuss problems of the VECs. The DCT felt that the members of higher social and economic group in the village have limited scope to wield power in the VECs. Therefore, members of upper strata seemed to be least interested in the VEC activities in the village. In the absence of proper communication system between the DCT and VECs and lack of transport facilities, the DCT found it difficult to provide proper guidance and supervision to the VECs at the village level.

Constitution / Reconstitution of VECs

The reconstitution of VECs carried out in 1993 and 1994 aimed at reactivation of VECs mostly through replacement of inactive members by more active persons. Guidelines for reconstitution of VECs issued by the BEP Sitamarhi from time to time were followed during the process of constitution. Other important changes made during reorganisation of VECs were related to dropping of guardian members whose children have left the school and members who were living outside the village. New members representing youth and women (and Mahila Samooh) and educationist among the villagers were included in the reconstituted VECs.

Profile of VEC Members

The average number of members in a VEC was 18, of which 14 were men and 4 were women. The number of VEC members ranged between 12 to 24. 55% of the VEC members were more than 40 years and 48% below 40 years of age. 55% were Matric and above, 27% members from upper castes group, 44% from Backward castes, 21% from Dalit and 8% were minorities. One third of the VEC members were engaged in agriculture, 17% each were service holders and labourers, 11% were engaged in petty business and 21% were either unemployed, retired or engaged in household work respectively.

The profile of the VEC members revealed that more than three fourth were men, more than half of them were adults above 40 years of age. Majority were having matriculations and above. The representation of different caste groups/communities was satisfactory. More than half of them were engaged in agriculture and labour.

The membership pattern of VECs has shown that in each VEC there were on an average four persons interested in education, two teachers, four women, two Dalit members, one from minorities and five from OBC.

The awareness of VEC members about the objectives of VEC was limited to areas of co-operation in school activities only, such as helping in enrolment, attendance and checking of drop outs of students, monitoring of teachers, construction/repairs and maintenance of school building and distribution of educational materials. Only one of the VEC reported supervision of NFE centre as one of the objectives of the VEC.

It was reported that twelve VECs were engaged in activities like checking dropouts, maintenance of school building, tree plantation and organisation of cultural and sports programmes in schools. Remaining eight VECs did not report their involvement in any educational activity in the school and the village.

VEC Meetings

It was reported that monthly VEC meetings were not being organised regularly in all the sample VECs. In four VECs the average attendance of VEC members was upto 6, in six VECs it ranged between 7 to 10 and in ten VECs the average attendance was more than 10 out of average 18 members. The attendance of women in VEC meetings was negligible in some blocks.

Most of the issues discussed in the VEC meetings were related to school activities like raising of enrolment, attendance, checking of dropouts, care of the school building, distribution of educational material and tree plantation respectively.

Shortcomings of VEC :

In many cases VECs were formed on paper by the block level officials rather than through the Gram Sabha. It was also observed that caste, rather than ability and interest of the person was given consideration while making selection. Many women and Scheduled castes members were not aware of their membership of VEC. Training of VEC members was conducted mostly through holding village level meetings. Initially the VEC members were very active in Bihar Education Project programme mainly because of hopes of getting some employment. In the absence of clear guidelines, monitoring and supervision of VEC, the members were in quandry about their role and responsibility in VEC.

Emergence of VSS

The VEC formed according to the earlier notification of 1988 by the State government suffered from the basic problem of the members being nominated by the Block Education Officer (BEO) and of the Mukhiya being the President. During 1991 to 1992, BEP restructured the character of the VECs. The President is now directly elected by the Gram Sabha and the Mukhiya is not necessarily the President.

Now Vidyalaya Shiksha Samiti has been formed as per Bihar State Vidyalaya Shiksha Samiti Act, 2000. The fifteen members of Vidyalaya Shiksha Samiti for the primary, middle and basic schools would be as follows:

(a) Parent Member nominated through Aam Sabha - 9.

(b) Non-parent members from Aam Sabha - 3.

(c) Nominated member by Mukhiya/Chairman/ Notified Committee / Municipality Corporation - 2.

(d) Headmaster of the school would be member - 1.

One third of the members should be female. Either Chairman or Secretary must be female. The duration of VSS office bearers is three years. It is registered by the Block Education Extension Officer. There is a Vidyalaya Shiksha Samiti development fund. The fund account is operated in a nationalised bank or Post Office. There is a provision to capacity building / development of members of Vidyalaya Shiksha Samiti, VSS has power to sanction the casual leave of Headmaster. The main function of the VSS is to monitor and supervise the school related works and report to the senior officers. To assist in enrolment and preparation of Bal Panji each year. VSS has right to supervise the mid-day meal / food and protshahan Bhatta to the students. In addition to these work VSS fixes the opening and closing time for the schools. The Samiti also takes decision other work for the spread of elementary education.

Role of BEP in the working of VSS

Bihar Education Project provides grants to the VSS for the construction of schools, toilets and handpump. It imparts school development grant of Rs. 2000 to each VSS. Rs. 5000/- is also given as repair and maintenance grant annually. This grant may be upto Rs. 7500/- as per requirement. Rs. 50,000/- is also given to VSS where no finance has given under Operation Black Board Scheme. Monitoring is also done by the BEP but monitoring work is lacking. District level officers are in touch with BEP. They are supposed to impart training to the VEC members as well as Mukhiya and Ward members. The training of VSS is supposed to be provided by the District Institute of Education and Training (DIET) but unluckly most of the district of Bihar do not have a DIET.

BEP sponsored diagnostic study project to the institution for the 17 districts in Bihar, where BEP was not working. This was done to implement Sarva Shiksha Abhiyan, which is an attempt to universalize elementary education by community ownership of the school system. It is a response to the demand for quality education. The SSA programme is also an attempt to provide an opportunity for improving human capabilities to all children, through provision of community owned quality education in a mission mode.

In 2001 the formation of the VSS started in the State. 16 VSS each have been formed in the Begusarai and Khagaria district each.

Profile of VSS members

The profile of VSS members of Begusarai and Khagaria districts is mentioned below :

Table 1: Genderwise distribution of VSS members

Gender	Begusarai	Khagaria
Male	55%	60%
Female	45%	40%

Most of the members of Vidyalaya Shiksha Samiti were male.

Table 2: Category-wise distribution of members

Caste	Begusarai	Khagaria
General	50%	12.5%
SC	11%	18.75%
OBC	38.80%	68.75%

Half of the VSS members belong to General category in Begusarai while majority of the members belong to OBC.

Table 3: Occupation wise distribution of VSS members

Occupation	Begusarai	Khagaria
Farming	40.0%	67.50%
Business	8.80%	3.75%
Service	1.30%	-
Others (Labours, domestic work)	50.10%	28.75%

As per above table the occupations of VSS members were farming, business, service and other domestic work. Half of the VSS members were in other category in Begusarai while majority of the members in Khagaria were in farming occupation.

Activities of VSS

The VSS is required to undertake various activities to perform its prescribed role in educational development of the village. Important activities of the VSS include survey of educational needs of the village, preparation of short / long term educational development plans and drawing up plans for the village primary schools/ Adult education /NFE centre, Aganwari centre etc. It has to undertake enrolment drive take steps for retention and motivate the guardians for enrollment their non school going children. It has to supervise and monitor the functioning of the school, AE/NFE centres in the village and will ensure creation of adequate educational facilities and infrastructure through community participation. It has to mobilise the community for educational planning in the village. It has to network youth and women social workers with AE and NFE programmes. It has to send reports to the higher authorities about the performance of school teachers and AE/NFE instructors.

The activities of VSS is discussed with the help of the following :

Table 4 : Frequency of VSS meeting

Duration	Begusarai (%)	Khagaria (%)
Twice a month	13.80	6.25
Once a month	40.0	88.75
Once in 2 months	7.50	2.50
Once in 3 months or above	35.0	1.25
No meeting	3.80	1.25

This table reveals that meetings was irregular. In Khagaria meetings were being organized once in a month. However some of the members complained that no meeting was held as yet in both the districts. During the field visit it appeared that proceedings of the meeting were not maintained properly. Less than half members of VSS of Begusarai reported that meeting is held once in a month.

Table 5 : Presence of members in meeting

Presence	Begusarai	Khagaria
100%	17.50	33.75
50%	73.80	51.25
25%	5.00	15.00
Not known	3.80	0.0

This table indicates that 50% members attend the meeting in both the district. Some of the VSS members had lost their enthusiasm. They were expecting honorarium for VSS work. Consequently the presence of members in the meeting was less than quorum.

Table 6 : Decision procedure in meeting

	Begusarai	Khagaria
By concensus	83.80	93.75
By majority	12.50	2.50
By some members	3.80	3.75

This table highlights that decision was taken by all as it was reported by most of the members in Begusarai and Khagaria districts. Almost all the members accepted that decision taken by majority but approximately 4% reported that decision was taken under pressure of some one.

Table 7 : Work undertaken after taking decision in the meeting

	Begusarai	Khagaria
Almost all decision	23.80	48.75
Most decision	21.30	28.75
Some decisions	38.80	22.50
No work	16.30	0.0

This table points out that work is done as per decision in the meeting. Approximately one fourth respondents from Begusarai and about half of the respondents from Khagaria reported that work is undertaken after decision taken in the meeting. 21.30% respondents from Begusarai and 28.75% respondents from Khagaria reported most of the decision while 38.80% respondents from Begusarai and 22.5% from Khagaria reported that some of the decision were implemented while some of the members from Begusarai reported no work was done as per decision taken by VSS members.

Table 8: Efforts made by the VSS to secure people's participation

Activities	Begusarai	Khagaria
Made villagers aware of education	70.00	81.42
Made door to door canvassing	73.80	82.85
Enrolment	92.50	95.71
Retention	86.30	86.25
Prabhat pheri	20.00	78.75
Bal Mela	17.50	43.75

Majority of VSS members reported that they have taken different steps to increase enrolment and retention. Mostly members moved from door to door for this. Prabhat pheri and Bal Mela were also organized in several cases for this work.

VSS has been playing an important role in improving educational environment of the school. Some places Secretary of VSS used to teach in the school as there was shortage of teachers in the school. VSS arranged some para teachers in some of the schools in Begusarai district. VSSs have been creating awareness among children and parents regarding educational development in the village. Monitoring the attendance of teachers in consultation of guardians is an important activity of VSS. Sometimes VSS arrange classes on its own initiative. They take some donation for the school building. Small problems are resolved with the active co-operation of VSS members. Its members request education officers to inspect the schools. VSS members approach MLA, M.P. regarding the problems of the schools. They arrange fund for the toilet from Panchayats. Moreover they arranged for unemployed educated youths of the village to take classes in the school without claiming remuneration.

Problems of Vidyalaya Siksha Samiti (VSS)

VSS members of the urban schools do not send their children to the government schools. Although their kids are enrolled in the schools but it is only for midday meal. They collect grain from the government schools but send their children to the private schools.

The process for the formation of VSS was completed in most of the cases but some places influential people came with arms and muscle men. They pressurized the selection process. VSS meeting is not organized regularly. Even proceedings of the meeting are not maintained properly. It appeared that members of VSS had lost their enthusiasm. This is why the presence of members in the meeting was less than quorum. They were expecting honorarium for working for VSS.

VSS members have not been imparted any training to enable them to perform their job effectively. This was the case both in rural and urban areas. Due to lack of training VSS members were more concerned with rights rather than duties This is why teachers complained that VSS members were creating pressure on the teachers and sometime they disturb them. Members of VSS were not aware about their rights and duties. In the Urban areas 60% VSS members were ignorant about the role and responsibilities of the VSS.

Decision taken by VSS members was not implemented at grass-root level. Usually only some of the decision were implemented. 17% respondents reported that no work was done to implement the decisions in the meeting.

Most of the VSS members tried to raise the enrolment of children in the school. They have done door to door contact for the retention of the students.

73% members reported that poverty is the main reason behind the non-enrolment and dropout of the students in the age group of 6-14 years. Half of the VSS members were either dissatisfied with the teaching system in the schools. Majority of the VSS members from Urban area were dissatisfied with the teaching learning system in the school.

Most of the VSS members from both rural and urban were not aware of the Sarva Shiksha Abhiyan. Irregularity of meeting and poor participation is a big hurdle in the smooth functioning of the VSS in Bihar. Generally it has been noticed that the meetings are only organized on paper and the signature of the members are procured later on. Even record / proceedings of the meeting was not maintained properly.

There should have been ten meetings in a year according to Bihar State Vidyalaya Shiksha Samiti Act 2000. However, the number of meetings actually held were less than the required number. In the urban area not more than six meetings were held while large proportion of the respondents in rural areas reported upto three meetings, most of them in urban area reported three to six meetings.

In most of the VSS meetings not more than one third members remain present. The rest used to engage in their own agirucultural work. Even if a member is free, he does not consider it important to participate in it. The excuse is that meeting hours are not convenient.

Similarly 25% to 50% members attend the meeting. This is why the presence of members in the meeting was less than quorum. There is an urgent need to bring some change in this direction as it is generally found that in the VSS meetings members do not turn up on one pretext or the other. Therefore, all the decision are not taken by majority.

It was observed that there was non availability of fund to the vidyalaya Shiksha Samiti. Some of the members of VSS reported that there was no money in Samiti for the development of the schools. They complained that VSS is just a show piece.

Shortcomings

There was no VSS in Pahsara, Sanjat and Gopalpur village in Begusarai district. In some of the schools VSS were not functioning properly. Formation of VSS played a havoc in some of the schools. A murder took place in one of the schools in Begusarai district. At the time of formation of Committee someone came with arms and musclemen. Teachers were scared. In some places some villagers wanted to be members of VSS because as they were expecting some allowances. Now members have become disillusioned. They do not attend meeting. In most of the schools meeting does not take place regularly. Quorum is not complete and registers are not maintained.

Due to lack of training, VSS members did not know their functions under VSS Act. Some of the members reported that VSS has been formed for the sake of VSS. Members were not taking any interest in the educational activity in the village. Majority of the VSS members were least involved in educational activities. There was no action plan with the VSS for initiating any better performance of school activity and mobilizing community participation for the development of education in the villages.

Suggestions for better performance

VSS members should be imparted training to enable them to perform their job effectively. Appropriate training facilities should be created at the block level for this purpose. Quality of training should be maintained so that VSS members can be helpful in planning, managing, monitoring and implementing other educational programmes in the village.

It must be ensured that all the VSSs hold their monthly meetings regularly and keep proper record of the proceedings. Care should be taken to improve attendance of VSS members to make a critical review of its performance and plan for next month.

Immediate and appropriate follow up activities should be initiated to execute the decision of the meetings at the grass root level. VSS should be linked with TLC, voluntary organization, development programmes, components of Sarva Shiksha Abhiyan as well as district office of Education department. Women member of the VSSs can be empowered through launching Mahila Samakhya programme.

Management Information System (MIS) should be further strengthened to monitor and coordinate VSSs.

Mal practices in the distribution of midday meal through fake enrolment of VSS Wards should be stopped. Students of private school should not be given midday meal from government schools on the basis of false enrolment.

Immediate steps should be taken to form VSS in the schools where they do not exist. In the existing VSS efforts should be made to nominate members who are sincere.

No formal training has yet been provided to any member of any VSS. Thus immediate steps should be taken to train the VSS members. Training should be provided to VSS members in a regular manner so that they can sustain the inputs of their training.

The VSS must prepare its quarterly plan of action and implement it accordingly. Immediate and appropriate follow up activities should be taken upto translate decision of meeting into action.

At present the school environment is not attractive due to multiple reasons. VSS must ensure that they will change the prevailing situation with the help of community. Government on its part should also look for suitable mechanism through which the VSS and the community can be actively involved.

Although VSS members admit that they are working for rise in enrollment and retention, the situation at the ground level is not satisfactory. It is high time for them to recognize the gravity of the problem and work in a realistic manner.

None of the VSS had yet opened a separate account in bank. This delay forbids them from formally taking any donation from any villager or agency which is interested in the development of school. It will also create a problem for them to utilize the development fund provided by the State government.

The proxy culture in VSS should be immediately stopped. It discourages the actual spirit of people's participation in educational affair, especially of women.

It has been observed that in recent years due to formation of many local bodies at the grass root level, the village atmosphere has become more politicised. Serious efforts should be made to form and maintain VSS a non political body otherwise it will totally violate the purpose of its formation.

VSS should establish and strengthen inter-sectoral linkages with NFE centres, ICDS, TLC, NGOs and with other development programmes of the villages.

Overview

The concept of community participation is not new to the field of education. People have always shown keen interest and have come forward for the cause of education. They are known to have made significant contribution, individually or collectively, for educational upliftment in the society. Village people have always been interested and involved in creation of schooling facilities for their children through voluntary effort or government action.

The BEP has emphasized training of VEC office-bearers and members to build their capabilities for playing effective role in the project. It revealed that large number of VEC office bearers are members were untrained in Sitamarhi district. Further the duration of training seemed to be inadequate to equip the VECs to take up the great task of planning managing and implementing the educational programme in the villages. So far as meeting of Village Education Committee is concerned. It was observed that most of the VECs were neither meeting regularly nor keeping proper records of proceedings of such meetings.

With the participation of VEC in school activities, there was visible improvement in the enrolment, retention and drop out rate of boys and girls of primary schools in general as well as from weaker sections. There was also certain improvement in the regularity and timely arrival of primary school teachers in the schools. There was lack of viable inter-sectoral linkage between the VEC and different components of the BEP and the development programmes in the village.

Vidyalaya Shiksha Samiti is an improvement over the Village Education Committee in Bihar. Now Vidyalaya Shiksha Samiti has been formed as per Bihar State Vidyalaya Shiksha Samiti Act, 2000.

Vidyalaya Shiksh Samiti (VSS) plays an important role to monitor the functioning of school teachers. It helps in creating educational environment in the area but also it helps in bringing teachers- parents together. Many VSSs have taken complete charge of school and it has been observed that the result and overall performance of such schools have improved a lot. It helped in the educational development through the community participation which was driving up due to take over of schools by the government.

Although formation of VSS in the school is a praiseworthy effort by the government, it could not deliver the goods as desired. The training input for the VSS members was very weak. They could not participate in the micro planning and other programmes for the school education. Despite financial crunch many VSS members taught students without taking any payment from them. Irregularity of meeting and poor participation is a big hurdle in the smooth functioning of VSS in Bihar. There is need to monitor and evaluate the overall activities of VSS. Action Research can be very helpful to solve the problems of VSS in Bihar.

REFERENCES

Govinda, R. and Diwan Rashmi (2003) : Community Participation and Empowerment in Primary Education, Sage Publications, New Delhi.

Kumar, Niraj (2002) : A Diagnostic Study of Khagaria District (under Sarva Shiksha Abhiyaan), Sulabh Institute of Development Studies, Patna.

Kumar, Somesh (2002): Methods for Community Participation - A complete Guide for Practitioners, Vistaar Publications, New Delhi.

Lal, Manohar (1995): Village Education Committee in Ranchi and Sitamarhi, Concurrent Evaluation of Bihar Education Project Council during 1994-95, A. N. Sinha Institute of Social Studies, Patna.

Pandey, Rajkumar (2002) : A Diagnostic Study of Begusarai District (Under Sarva Shiksha Abhiyaan), Sulabh Institute of Development Studies, Patna.

Sachchidananda (2000) : Role of VEC in Community Participation So Far, Sulabh Institute of Development Studies, Patna.

8

EDUCATION AND EMPOWERMENT OF WOMEN THROUGH MAHILA SAMAKHYA

R. K. Pandey

It is universally recognised that education can work as a positive intervention in raising the status of women. But in most developing countries low status and rigid socio-cultural practices deny women their basic right. Education is a necessary but not sufficient condition for raising their status. The critical issue is providing more income to women and also give them control over income. The essence of development is to create conditions for women to live in dignity and to meet their basic needs, give them freedom from violence and exposure to information and education. The fact that most women in villages and urban slums are so caught up in daily struggles for fuel, fodder and wages that they have no time for anything else. They are kept away from the decision making processes. They are also systematically robbed of their confidence and paralysed by their dim self image.

The Mahila Samakhya reaches out to rural poor women in thousands of villages in U.P., Gujarat, Andhra Pradesh, Karnatakka and Bihar. Mahila Samakhya has mobilized women to send their daughters to school. Another major outcome is women's participation in local self government institutions. A large number of women across the country have contested and won elective posts in the Panchayat system. Educaiton remains the thrust of the conceptual framework of the programme. Acquiring self confidence, being able to deal with authority knowledge of health issues feeling more command over one's life and shedding helplessness, some reading and writing have empowered women all along the line specially grass root facilitators, women leaders and functionaries.

All over the world, the movement for improving women's status has always emphasised education as the most significant instrument for social change. The social reformers of the 19th century tried to use education more to ameliorate the position of women socially. They were able to awaken the conciousness of the nation to the evils of child marriage, sati, polygamy, enforced widowhood, dowry system etc. As the new western education which developed during the 19th century invariably meant "a method of earning" and women were not required to earn, it was not necessary for women to be educated. Learning to do household work was sufficient for her and so the parents were not keen to incur any expenditure in educating the girls till very recently.

During the present century, the country has made spectacular progress in promoting the cause of women. The female literacy rate went up 33% in 2001 in Bihar. But there is a wide gap between male and female literacy. There is uneven rate of progress in all levels of education between different states. There is vast disparity between education of girls in rural and urban areas. There is a big gap between enrolment of girls belonging to the Scheduled caste / tribe and higher castes. Girls belonging to Scheduled castes and tribes are also lagging behind boys in their own community.

The Bihar Education Project was launched in 1991, with a view to revitalize the sagging spirit of the educational institutions of the State. The project is committed to the universalization of primary education and the systematic and scientific upgradation of the quality of 'education for all' by 2000. This goal can be achieved only through the complete and active involvement of the community. To ensure community participation BEP makes use of various strategies like environment building in the villages; involving people in activities like micro level planning and school mapping, constituting village education committees and entrusting them with the responsibility of construction and maintenance of school buildings and selection of teachers, encouraging the formation of women's groups and encouraging them for enrolment of children (specially girls) monitoring of schools and supervising Jagjagi and Bal Jagjagi Kendras.

Women empowerment through Mahila Samakhya is the one of the most important components of the Bihar Education Project.

Mahila Samakhya

Mahila Samakhya believes in empowering women through education. The term 'Samakhya' means 'communication between equals' thus the programme proposes to use the medium of education as a platform for women's equality. The programme creates a space for women to come together and share their 'self' without fear of ridicule or doubt. It believes in the power of collective decision making and aims to inculcate a positive self image in women. The programme came into existence on the recommendation of the National Policy on Education (1986) with the aim of mobilizing women for education, development and social change. The main objective of Mahila Samakhya programme is to empower girls and women particularly of those who belong to deprived communities through education. The agency which looks after this programme in Bihar is Bihar Education Project Council (BEP). Now Mahila Samakhya (M.S.) is blossoming into a movement, with membership of about 60231 women in the project districts.

Mahila Samakhya has very well defined objectives which has been a strong guiding force for the programme.

- Instil self confidence and create a positive self image in women.
- Create an environment where women can appreciate the importance and need for education.
- Inculcate an interest for education in their life.

Mahila Samakhya programme is being implemented in Rohtas, West Champaran, Muzaffarpur, Sitamarhi, Darbhanga, Bhojpur and Gaya districts in Bihar.

In this study we have covered the programme in Rohtas and Muzaffarpur. The status of Mahila Samakhya programme in Rohtas and Muzaffarpur upto March 2004 is given below :

	Rohtas	Muzaffarpur
Blocks covered	3	5
Panchayats covered	53	105
Villages covered	357	410
Number of Mahila Samoohs	370	572
Number of Savings Samoohs	404	504
Number of Samooh members	11986	13308
Trained Samoohs	272	282
Amount of internal savings	-	25,51490
Number of Sahyoginis	28	32
Number of Jagjagi Kendra	89	259
Number of Bal Jagjagi Kendras	40	162
Number of Girls in Jagjagi Kendras	1547	7305
Number of Women in Jagjagi Kendra	1270	1117
Number of Girls in Bal Jagjagi Kendras	707	2549
Number of Boys in Bal Jag jagi Kendras	638	2448

[contd...]

[contd...]

	Rohtas	**Muzaffarpur**
Mahila Shikshan Kendra	1	1
Mahila Kutir	40	17
Number of Information Centres	-	8
Formed Kishori Manch	127	103
Girls in the Manch	3309	1900
No. of Balika Vihar	-	6
Trained Kishori	727	944
Total enrolment villages	111	54
No. of Mobile Libraries	28	31
Trained Women Masons	10	36

Mahila Samakhya in Rohtas District

The Mahila Samakhya was started in 1992. The field of operation of Mahila Samakhya (M.S.) programmes are Chenari, Sheosagar and Sasaram blocks of the district. The total covered villages in these blocks are 357. Altogether 370 groups were formed out of which 150 were of Scheduled caste groups while the rest were groups of other Backward caste women. The total number of Schedule caste women was 8700. There is a district core team, 2 district trainers, 30 Sahyoginis in the Mahila Samakhya at the district level. 40 Mahila Kutirs, 1 Mahila Shikshan Kendra and 1 Field centre are working in the district. There is great emphasis on savings in the Mahila Samoohs. Training is one of the key activities of Mahila Samakhya. The objective of the training programme is to help the trainees internalise enabling attitudes and values; to assist them to understand and critically analyse prevalent socio-economic and political structures and to encourage . ative leadership in society. Mahila Samakhya anizes 3 day training programme for Mahila Samooh, 2 day camp for Sakhi training, 5 day for Kishori training and 15 day training for Saheli. In addition to training, 10 days refresher course is also organized for the

Saheli. The Samakhya organizes training for Balmitra and legal awareness for capacity building of the villagers and officials at the grass root level.

Activities of the Mahila Samakhya

There are many programmes for the empowerment of women by the Mahila Samakhya, important among those programmes are educational, formation of Kishori Manch, Bal Mela, Kishori Mela, Curbing violence against women, elimination of dowry, immunization camps, awareness about government programmes, taking loan from NABARD, training for capacity building, health and sanitation programme etc. The main focus of educational programme is on vocational training for self reliance among girls and women. These programmes created demand for Sulabh Shauchalaya among women. Mahila Samakhya has organised training of women masons for the construction of toilets at the village and district level. In addition to training, it created an environment for the self employment opportunities to the Group members. Mahila Samakhya Rohtas promoted networking of Samooh with NABARD schemes. It created awareness about schemes implemented by Government and non-Government organizations.

Mahila Samakhya workers explained the benefits from these schemes to the Dalit women. Now they have become self reliant and changed their attitude towards self employment. Now Dalit women are keen about education. Consequently there is increase in enrolment and reduction in drop-out rate. Initiatives of Mahila Samakhya have changed the attitude and behaviour of teachers. The attendance of teachers in the school has already improved. Dalit women are aware about their own rights they have started paying attention to health and sanitation.

Women's Participation in Panchayati Raj

Dalit women participated in Panchayat election and now they are getting benefit from Government programmes like old age pension and Annapurna yojana. The most important benefit which emerged due to the efforts of Mahila Samakhya is freedom from the exploitation of money lenders. Dalit women have been empowered through these programmes like Group formation, organisation of women, knowledge sharing, attendance in the meeting of Gram Sabha and Aam Sabha (village meeting and general meeting) to provide training, consultation with officers in the different department, information sharing with block officials regarding Government programmes and benefit from these programmes, demand for appropriate wage, prohibition on early marriage, awareness about health and sanitation among adolescent girls and women. Now empowered women are workers of Mahila Samakhya at the local level like Balmitra, Saheli and Karate trainers.

M. S. workers have suggested measures for checking the atrocities on Dalit women. These are organisation and unity, training and information about new things, awareness and construction of sulabh shauchalaya in Dalit locations. Elimination of caste and class discrimination, economic assistance, appropriate wage, employment opportunities, awareness about education, critical thinking among adolescent girls and women, gender sensitization, decision making capacity etc. They highlighted the hurdles in the empowerment of Dalit women. These are caste discrimination, poor access to government officials, no attention to Dalit voice under Panchayati Raj, no importance to schemes prepared by the Dalit women, lack of education, feudal attitudes, low self esteem etc.

They felt that Dalit women should get guidance for vocational training and for small business like making potato chips, detergents, construction of Sulabh toilets, compost and vermiculture. Reasons for the spread of diseases should be explained to them.

Educational Impact

Mahila Shikshan Kendra of Mahila Samakhya plays

a vital role for educational development of drop-out girls particularly of the Scheduled castes and the deprived sections of the society. It creates awareness and provides vocational training for women empowerment. Adolescent girls from the Scheduled castes are being trained in this Kendra. During the eight month training they are given a stipend of Rs. 40 per month and two sets of dresses, books and writing materials. After training they are engaged in awareness generation and setting up Kishori Manch in the village. They work for curbing child marriage. The important consequences of Mahila Shikshan Kendra training are spread of education, employment and awareness which work for empowerment. Majority of learners are drop-outs or those who are out of school due to poverty and ignorance. But now some of them are planning to join the National Institute of Open Schooling Study Centres. Mahila Samakhya work has led to a rise in enrolment and demand for education. There is reduction in drop-out due to the involvement of grass root level organizations (Mahila Samooh of Mahila Samakhya). Scheduled caste girls received training in judo-karate, cycling and games. Such training has created great impact on SC adolescent girls and now they are self employed in sewing centres and working as Saheli, Balmitra, Sahyogini and Aganwadi sevika. Now they are imparting knowledge about the evils of child marriage and making the people aware of their legal rights and duties.

Empowerment through Micro Credit

Members of Mahila Samooh have formed savings Groups in the villages of Chenari, Sheosagar, Sasaram blocks in Rohtas district. They have deposited money in SHG accounts in the Bank. The amount is more than Rs. 50,000/- in a group. Members of an SHG take loan from the account for buying cattle, poultry, goatry, and for shop-keeping and share cropping. One Sakhi, Lakshminiya Devi of Adimapur village started a tea stall on the G.T. Road in a thatched hut. Now she is selling rice, bread, tadka and other things in the stall. This was possible because of a loan of Rs. 500 from SHG account. Now her husband and sons are engaged running the small hotel. Her ambition is to expand this hotel on G.T. road. This programme has created zeal for entrepreneurship among rural women.

Capacity building through Mahila Samakhya

Capacity building of the poor, deprived and Dalit is very important for the Mahila Samakhya for the empowerment of women. Training at different levels of the programme, whether for the Sahayogini, Samooh or Sakhi is an effective tool to help women in recognizing and building up their self worth and confidence. These training programmes have raised their self image and led to personal growth. It has awakened the potentialities and skills of women through training in Mahila Samakhya by a participatory approach, where the trainer and trainees grow together by learning from each other.

Mahila Shikshan Kendra plays a vital role in capacity building among 15-35 age group of adolescent girls and women. It creates awareness which is necessary for women empowerment. The Mahila Shikshan Kendra (MSK) conducts classes for the educational upgradation, personality development capacity building for different vocations. In addition to these it provides training in karate, cycling and catering.

Due to the capacity building through Mahila Samakhya programme, Smt. Sitara Devi became Ward member of Kathdihri village of Sheosagar block in Rohtas district. She has been working for the empowerment of Scheduled caste women at the Panchayat level. Given below is a brief description of the building of this women leader.

Smt. Sitara Devi, wife of Shri Vijai Ram belongs to the Nat caste. She is 30 years old and educated upto Matric. She is landless. Her husband sells tobacco on a cart and is also a share cropper. She lives in a remote village Kathdihri under Sheosagar block of Rohtas district. She is the Saheli of Jagjagi kendra. 1 to 5th class are covered in 3 years at the Jagjagi kendra. She got training in two phases and attends refresher course after every three months. She admitted 5 girls of the Nat caste at Jagjagi Kendra and sent them to Mahila Shikshan Kendra. Due to her association with the Mahila Samakhya she was able to contest Panchayat election. She was elected Ward member and is doing very good work in Panchayat. Earlier some girls of the Nat caste were not married off by their parents. They were sold and engaged in dancing and singing. But now due to the efforts of Sitara Devi many girls are being married off by their parents. With the help from Mukhiya she got Indira Awas for Nat and Rabidas castes. She helped four old persons to get their pension.

She felt distressed at government officials not issuing caste certificates to Nats. This is why Nat caste is not able to enjoy facilities meant for Scheduled castes. She told the research team that Public Interest litigation has been filed in the Patna High Court. She is doing a lot for the benefit of Dalit adolescent girls and women. She is imparting education at the **Jagjagi Kendra**. She is helping Dalit women access government schemes. She helped Dalit women in Annapurna yojana and other programmes. She is making people aware of health, sanitation and personal hygiene. She has been helping women's group for the developmental work.

All these activities of Sitara Devi are the result of empowerment through Mahila Samakhya programme. Now she sends her daughter to the school. Her husband also cooperates in household work as she is busy with Jagjagi Kendra and Panchayat activities. Now she is engaged in development work in the village. People of all castes have faith in her. The future plan of Sitara Devi is to empower women with the help of Mahila Samakhya and to get recognition of Nat as a Scheduled caste in her area. This will enable them to get benefit from the government programmes meant for Scheduled castes.

Case Studies

1. Shivsagar is one of the three blocks of Rohtas district in which this Mahila Samakhya (M.S.) programme run. It is located 5 km west of district headquarter. Smt. Kasmira Devi (K.D.) a resident of Righia village in this block has been associated with the M.S. programme since 1992. A mother of seven children and a wife of an electrician working in Electricity Board used to find her life unsatisfying. She hails from a Dusadh caste and did not find any other field for development until she joined the M.S. Although all of her children had elementary education but only one could continue above the matriculation level. She herself has no formal education, may be due to her marriage at the tender age of 12 years.

In the year 1992, at a age of thirty seven she came in contact of a Sahayogni (cluster level M.S Worker) and two years later she received the training of Sakhi (village level M.S. Motivator) at the district headquarter. There she came in contact of Sister Sabeena, the then District Co-ordinator of M.S. programme and through her initiative she realised the exploitation which other women and girls of her village were subjected to in their every day life. Later she formed Taragan Self Help Group in her village in the year 1996. This has distributed a loan of more than Rs. 20,000 among its members. She has also visited Vaishali, Ranchi and Patna in connection to her training on different women issues and figures as a participant of M.S. International meet at Delhi in the year 2000.

She admitted that female infanticide was common in her village, irrespective of their caste some ten years ago. She even recalled how her own mother faced the curse of the family male members including her husband and father-in-law when she gave birth to her seventh daughter. She was forced by the male members to stop providing any liquid diet to the new born. In two days the baby died. She was just six years old at that time.

She still finds it hard to forget it. Her own experience and commitment for the M.S. programme made her start a campaign against this practice. On her initiative members of her committee spread this message among the villagers that those who will commit this act will not go free and the police will be informed.

But all was not so easy for her. In the initial stage villagers started a campaign against her. Stones and excreta were thrown on her house. She was prohibited from leaving her house and make any visit to block where M.S. meetings used to take place. Villagers used to accuse her of misleading other women and girls of the village by infusing new ideas about their rights. A false police case was also registered against her in the local police station with a view to compel her to stop her activities. On finding that she could not garner support in the village to overcome this crisis, she asked for support from the district level M.S. workers. She was also finding it hard to cope with the Police who from time to time started harassing her. In itself this issue was not small and the news reached Mr. Raghavan, the then State Programme Director (S.P.D.) of B.E.P. Mr. Raghavan wasted no time and visited the spot. He warned the Police that such behaviour will not be tolerated and they should instead support the real victim and a police inquiry was set up. With the visit of S.P.D. the whole scenario changed and gradually people started realising that it was not easy to stop this woman from making women aware of their rights. The people who were disturbing her belonged to Scheduled castes community but they were instigated by the upper caste people, mainly the Brahmin. She is happy today, as now no one dares to commit such inhuman act.

A number of complications arise when a girl is married at a very tender age. Early marriage leads to early pregnancy which is biologically bad for both the mother and the child. In several cases either of the two lose their life. But people are not concerned about these facts and they have different ideas to defend the tradition of child marriage. K. D. thinks that this practice is a big hurdle in the way of girl empowerment. Child marriage deprives girls from receiving formal education. Girls are only treated as a reserve pool of labour for domestic as well as agriculture work by the family members before their marriage.

Her mild persuasion to stop this practice yielded no results. So in the year 2000 she took a bold step against the prevalence of this practice. A Kahar family was going to arrange the marriage of their 9 years old daughter. On the marriage day K. D. along with her committee members reached the spot and started singing songs prepared by them on mike. These songs lambasted the evil effects of child marriage. Everybody was stunned at this move of a women coming from a deprived community with the support of a few followers. The family members and other relatives of the bridegroom became helpless. They were told that police has been already informed and the marriage will put them behind the bars. At last both the parties agreed to stop the marriage with an understanding that the marriage will again take place between the two when they attain the marriageable age. Everybody including K. D. then enjoyed the feast arranged for the marriage . She felt proud. She added that she will never forget that feast. Later the girl was admitted in a Jagjaji centre (non-formal girls education centre) and thus became a member of Kishori Manch. Her entry in Kishori Manch further boosted the morale of other girls who may otherwise were waiting to meet a similar fate.

She holds that one of the causes of mass poverty and deprivation of the Scheduled castes, especially the Musahar is that they consume liquor on a large scale. The problem becomes more severe when it is locally produced. A similar situation prevailed in her village where the Bind caste people used to make liquor out of Mahua. This was their traditional occupation and no one hitherto ever tried to stop them. K. D. realised that nothing substantial can be planned for the uplift of the

Scheduled castes unless this addiction is checked. People used to spend their hard earned family income on liquor but never bothered to encourage their women to contribute in the S.H.G. Thus the existence of the established S.H.G.'s was threatened due to the default in the subscription of its members.

One night, in a planned move members of Taragan S.H.G. made a raid in the houses of Bind caste people and caught three persons and handed them over to the local police. All the apparatus and raw materials meant for making liquor were destroyed. An FIR was also lodged against them by K. D. in the police station. But next day to her utter surprise all the three accused were set free by the police allegedly through illegal gratification.

This behaviour of the police shocked her. She was determined to face this challenge. This time she collected about fifty women and led a delegation directly to the D.S.P. Office and informed him about the whole episode. The D.S.P. was impressed by seeing her determination for this cause. The Officer in-charge of her village police station was asked to arrest all the three offenders within 12 hours and subsequently compliance of order was made. Since then, no one in the village dares to make mahua liquor. Even in some near by villages those Bind families who were involved in this occupation gave it up due to the fear of punishment. Now a large portion of S.H.G. saving comes from the money which otherwise would have gone for liquor. The conflict within the family over this issue has also evaporated.

Previously the attitude of police towards the Scheduled caste people used to be very repressive. Several incidents went unreported. When they came to the village, they took away by force goats and hen they from their houses. Any resistance meant physical torture. In some cases women and girls were sexually abused. Women belonging to Musahar community were an easy target for them. Looking back K. D. feels that now things were improving as these people are getting united through the formation of S.H.G. At the same time they are also aware of their legal rights with the help of the Sakhi and Sahayogni under M. S. programme. At Mahila Kutir such awareness meetings are arranged every week. Now these women have devised a mechanism in the form of pressure group with the formation of S.H.G. to protect their interest from their former exploiters.

Social environment is key for women empowerment. The M.S. programme puts more emphasis on this environment building. They not only target the elderly women but also approach young girls through Jagjaji centre and Kishori Manch for capacity building among them. This is a long process and require sustained efforts and supportive environment. But in case of young girls the entire exercise is futile once she is married. Many times it is not sure whether she gets similar environment at her in-laws home to carry out her activities. This issue raised a debate among the M.S. workers as they had no strategy to cope with this new situation. K. D. showed them a way out. She requested members of all the committees of her village to marry their sons and daughters only in such families who are already attached with similar committee in their own village. By adopting this approach the purpose of training imparted to a girl before her marriage will carry for ever. Similarly, by doing so, the sustainability of the programme and the desire to participate in it will remain intact.

Devotion for more than ten years in the M.S. programme has given K. D. a high respect in the organization. Now she is well known even outside her block as a champion fighting for the liberation of Scheduled castes women. She is now planning to grow vegetables on an experimental basis by taking land on rent from big farmers. This exercise will be jointly operated by all the members of the committee and profit will be equally shared among them. If the situation remains in her favour, she will start producing potato chips and other similar food products which can be easily sold out in near by markets. This idea she conceived because at present Scheduled castes women are gradually shifting from their traditional agricultural work due to increasing mechanization in this field. Apart from this they have also lost their employment avenues in crusher industry due to its closure in the near by areas. She is now much satisfied with her contribution for the betterment of her own community members particularly women by exploring employment venues in other areas. Reasons for hope in the context of over all development of Dalit are many for K. D. But at the same time she is aware of the fact that people like her are very few in M.S. On the whole she is optimistic about the future of these Dalit women.

2. Radhika, a poor Harijan women, resident of Muradabad, led a life of abject misery. The burden of a large family combined with the harassment of an alcoholic husband, had made Radhika age before her time. Desperate to make both her ends meet, she often had to resort to borrowing from her neighbours.

When Mahila Samakhya came to Muradabad, Radhika too became a member of the Samooh. In the beginning though, her participation in the Samooh meetings was negligible. Sahyogini Malathi recalls "*Radhika used to be incommunicative usually sitting in one corner and brooding. At times I would force her to speak up, sometimes she used to confide her troubles to me as to how she found it difficult to meet family expenses, how her husband spent all his money on liquor and often beat her up*".

So when the thrift and credit programme was introduced, the Sahyogini persuaded Radhika to become a member. In September 1998, Radhika took a loan of Rs. 700 from internal savings of the Samooh. This money she used to open a small tea shop just outside the village on the main road. Her shop was an instant hit in the area. Customers flocked to the little tea shop in large numbers. "That was the turning point in my life" - says Radhika with a smile.

Radhika's shop opens by 8 o'clock in the morning and by the time she closes her shop, it is usually 9 P.M. or later. She sells around Rs. 350-400 worth of tea every day. Other than tea - paan is another popular item in her shop. She feels that having a source of income has brought about a lot of changes in her life.

3. It was late winter afternoon. Shanti Devi was relaxing in her make shift home, after a hard days work. Just as she was dozing in a corner, the landlord's hefty henchman stormed into her room and dragged Shanti out, showering her with blows and kicks and abuses. Leaving her half concious, they then proceeded to seal the door to her house with mud and bricks.

Shanti knew that it was no use trying to stop the men. This was the landlord's way of reminding her that as a mere Harijan and a women, she had no right to go against his wishes.

Shanti is a Sakhi of the Mahila Samooh of Amta village. Ever since the Mahila Samakhya came into the village, with its message of women's power and equality, Shanti has been one of the most vociferous advocates of the programme raising issues on minimum wages, land rights and women issues and urging the villagers, especially the women, to protest against the oppression of the landlords. She thus succeeded in raising the ire of the upper classes of the village, who lost no opportunity of making life difficult for her.

During the heavy monsoon Shanti's house had collapsed, forcing the family to live in the cattle shed. The cattleshed had a single door, which opened into a narrow lane, where people tied their cattle. This made it difficult for Shanti to use the door, which opened out on the main road. It was coincidental that this road also led to the landlord's fields.

It was thus, that Shanti was thrown out of her house

and the door scaled. Shanti and her family members were left without shelter. Shanti approached the Samooh and asked for their support. The women got together and with the help of the Sahyogini mobilised women from Mahila Samoohs all over the Panchayat of Alampur. When the DCT heard of the incident, they were also eager to join hands with the Samoohs. A few days after the incident, a team of 82 women marched over to Amata and broke through the mud and brick seal and fixed a wooden door at the opening. But the police accompanied by the landlords men arrived on the scene and promptly locked the door, declaring that Shanti could not open the lock as the door was on disputed land.

It was a big blow to the women gathered at the spot, who were hoping to reinstall Shanti in her house. But they were not to be daunted. They decided to keep on their struggle contacting more women all over the block / district. They contacted the higher officials where necessary.

In time this brave struggle of a group of courageous women fighting for their basic rights, caught the notice of the State authorities. On making inquiries into the case they relised that the women were indeed putting up a fight for a just cause.

Thus, it was that on the 16th of March 1994, after six months of struggle, Shanti opened the door of her house. This was one of the major triumphs for Mahila Samakhya, Rohtas.

Mahila Samakhya in Muzaffarpur

Mahila Samakhya programme started in 1993 in Muzaffarpur. Five blocks i.e. Musahari, Bochha, Karhani, Gaighat, Aurai have been covered by the programme. There are 410 covered villages, 574 Mahila Samooh and 483 Savings groups. There are 12925 group members and Rs. 25,51,490 internal savings by the efforts of Mahila Samakhya. Altogether 32 Sahyoginis have been working in the Mahila Samakhya programme.

259 Jag Jagi Kendra and 162 Bal Jag Jagi Kendras have been working in 5 blocks. 7305 girls and 1020 women have been studying while 2549 girls and 2448 women boys are enrolled in Bal Jag Jagi Kendra.

Mahila Shikshan Kendra, Chandwara has 35 - 40 seats but there are 59 trainees. There are 5 Balika Vihars in Muzaffarpur district. This is centre for those girls who have never gone to school. Balika Vihar is not there in any other BEP district. Mahila Samakhya constructed 1692 toilets in collaboration with UNICEF. Major beneficiaries are people below the poverty line.

Social Impact

Previously women were not paying attention to health care. But due to constant efforts of Mahila Samakhya women came to know about the importance of immunization for the child and women. Now women go to immunize themselves and their children. Samooh members have been participating in pulse polio programme from last three years.

With the help from WHO, training programmes were organized at district and village level for members of Samooh. These trained members imparted training to the village women. The main focus in the training was change in sanitation habits awareness about effects of child marriage, precautionary measures for T.B., Malaria, HIV, AIDS and Blood cancer. They were also made aware about the precaution to be taken in pre and post natal stage.

Samooh members have stopped defecation on the road side by planting Tulsi plant. This was the case of Bhatoulia village in Mushahari block. Sahyogini Nirmala Devi played important part in creating better environmental sanitation in the village. She used to organize discussion among the Samooh members.

Economic impact

Promotion of savings by the group is a step for economic self reliance. The important aspect of this initiative is collective savings through Mahila Samooh. There are 277 savings group out of 374 groups in the Muzaffarpur district. They saved Rs. 28,50,000 through the groups. Now they are free from moneylenders. 429 women members started self employment, while 138 group started collective employment under which they purchased mango garden, engaged in fishery, and making of chura, rope and honey. Now they have been liberated from the debt and money lender both.

Production centre is run by the group in Mushahari village. In this women are building toilets in houses. The Executive Engineer of PHED visited this centre and was surprised to see women masons making toilets under the banner "*Stree Ban Gai Mistri*" (Women have become mason). Savitri reported that she has installed 300 toilets in the district. Now women masons are able to send their children to schools. She purchased one cycle for her elder son and opened a shop near her house for her husband. Now she is self reliant. Savitri reported that two women of her village got training for mason. Now there are 16 women masons in this district. The Executive Engineer disclosed that they were also going to start toilet construction. He asked for a message from Savitri. She holds that women do not have lower capacity than men. She advised him to involve women in his programme.

Many group members have been benefited from the Mahila Samakhya programme. Due to economic empowerment through savings women have been freed from the dependence on moneylenders, family and husband. Now women have something their own and now they can take their own decision about spending self earned income.

Mahila Samakhya took great interest in Sampoorna Gram Swarojgar Yojana consequently 212 groups qualified for loans. Rs. 2.5 lac per group was given to 16 groups. About 200 groups have received revolving fund of Rs. 10,000. Now group members have been engaged in vegetable and Bangle selling, making of *sattu* and *chura*, fish and cattle rearing.

Women Participation in Panchayati Raj

Panchayati Raj emanated from the Constitutional amendment no. 73 and 74 enacted in 1993. Awareness about Panchayati Raj system was spread by the Mahila Samakhya along with other programme. The main purpose behind this effort was to encourage the participation of women in forthcoming Panchayati Raj election. Information centre was opened for this purpose. Process of election, voting and idea regarding ballot paper and nomination paper was given to the group members by Sahyogini and other functionaries.

Group members selected 85 women for contesting election. Altogether 56 women won. 49 as Ward members 6 as members of Panchayat Samiti and two as Mukhiya and one Mukhiya got elected. Due to the constant efforts of group members people have been benefited by the construction of roads and Indira Awas Yojana. After election Scheduled caste women have been participating in the development work of the village. Smt. Krishna Devi of Shivraha Chaturbhuj village under Bochahan block became Ward member. She became member of women group during 1994. Now she is an empowered lady of village. She took up several works of rural development in the village. With the co-operation of Village Committee and Mukhiya she got pucca road built.

People are demanding the Indira Awas and handpump. She helped them to get Indira Awas and handpump. She got Jagjagi and Bal Jagjagi Kendra opened. In this way she promoted the advancement of Dalits and women in the village.

Efforts for freedom from exploitation and atrocities

Child marriage, wife beating, dowry death, remarriage, castigating widows as witches are the different kinds of atrocities on women. Mahila Samakhya took a praiseworthy initiative to curb these atrocities. Those involved in dowry death were given punishment due to efforts of Mahila Samakhya. They arranged to give right to the first wife and tried to rehabilitate the deserted wife. They provided dignity to women denounced as a witch. Mahila Samakhya adopted some strategies for this. They made the women/ adolescent girls aware by providing training in legal matters. For this Samooh members visit Police-station and court to know the legal process. Samooh members approached both the victims and guilty. Besides they associated the local people to solve the problems. Group members take assistance from police, administration, health and other related departments.

Issues solved through court were rape, dowry in Basoul village, exploitation on the name of marriage, in parati and turkey beating in Gobarsahi, rape after kidnapping in Mahanth Maniyari and other villages.

Issues solved by counselling in some villages were beating in Sakari Saraiya, rape in Chaklahad, extortion in Chaturi punas, torture by husband in Chakhasan, rape in Manika, marriage by cheating in Dhobaha, Non-payment of wages in chainpur bangra and beating in Balahiyan. Other issues were also solved by the Mahila Samakhya.

Monitoring and MIS

Monitoring is an integral part of the Mahila Samakhya Programme, and is carried out at different levels of the programme by the concurred staff. The stress is not so much on quantitative achievements as on the process of implementation. The social effect of the programme on women, in particular and on the programme at large, is more important. To monitor the progress at different levels of activities Sakhi, Sahyogini, and District Core Team (DCT) are responsible. Sakhi is responsible for arranging meetings, implementation of activities and monitoring at village level. At the cluster level the Sakhis keep in touch with each other on a regular basis for sharing their experiences and for planning out their activities. They are also responsible for issue based networking among samoohs. Monthly meetings of Sahyoginis are held at the District Mahila Samakhya Resource Centres, to plan out activities and strategies for the coming month. Reflection sessions / meetings of the DCT are held every 3 months at the State level. The sharing of experiences and views and the process of taking decision as a group helps to foster the team spirit which is a very important aspect of the programme. The Mahila Samakhya personnel are required to evaluate their own performance. Besides, inter cluster evaluation by Sahyoginis and inter district evaluation by core team members and BEP representatives are also carried out from time to time.

Impact on Education

The role of the samoohs does not end with the enrolment of children and the distribution of text books to primary schools. The samoohs are also entrusted with the task of the constant monitoring of the schools with a view to reduce the drop out rates (especially for girls). This also keeps the teachers alert and regular.

The samooh members are also active participants of the Vidyalaya Shiksha Samiti (VSS). To ensure community participation in the education process the Bihar Education Project stresses on the formation of VSS in every village. These VSSs are responsible for the construction and maintenance of school buildings. All funds for construction and maintenance are handed over to the VECs. This has given rise to a lot of undesirable 'politics' within the groups as vested interests have emerged concerning the control of the funds.

Altogether 111 in Rohtas and 54 in Muzaffarpur districts are total enrolment villages where all the 6 - 14 age group children are enrolled. Mahila samooh played an important role in the enrolment and retention in primary schools. This created good impact on general education.

Vision for the Future

The main aim of Mahila Samakhya is not only to

create awareness but to sustain this awareness among women. Those who have already been awakened must awake others. Organization should get feedback regularly and awakened women should be attached with the Mahila Samakhya. The need for uniting small groups into a big organization was realized. Consequently Federation from strong groups was formed in Muzaffarpur and Rohtas the districts. Strong group was identified on the basis of index at the cluster level meetings. In this way, they formulated rules and regulation for the federation. Formation of federation is a priaseworthy initiative which will provide backward and forward linkages to the savings groups. This would be helpful for the sustainability of the women group and savings groups. In the long run it will provide the benefit of institutional mechanism to groups and savings groups of the villages.

Mahila Samakhya programme is moving towards its independent identity in Rohtas and Muzaffarpur districts. The process is as yet slow but the District Core Team (DCT) has ensured greater clarity on the issue since October '99 at every level. The following understanding has been created among the DCT members and is being percolating to the groups at village level :

- Phasing out is a crucial part of the empowerment process and leads to the ultimate goal.
- Group identity and its operational principles will not be influenced in the process of federating groups into the central power structure. The groups shall continue to function as all the time.
- A smooth bottom up structure is to be evolved to federate groups into the central structure which will function as the facilitating body, a role currently being played by the District Core Team.
- No major infrastructure will be build up at federation level, emphasis will be given to group

promotion and its community infrastructure building within group control and entity.

- Federation will be registered under society registration act of the State and shall function as a non-profit making institution. This organisation shall facilitate group to promote enterprise and on profit at group and individual member capacity.
- A three tier structure is under review i.e. Tier - I : Group selects a group representative at (Tier - II) Sankul level (sankul is restructured at Panchayat level) - Panchayat - Sankul selects a (Tier - III) district level general body. General body appoints an executive committee to take care of the day to day activities of the women' organization at large.
- The District Core Team has initiated dialogue and awareness on phase out process and consulting the groups on its various issues i.e. structure, function and relation, constitution, capacity and sustainability issues.

Phase out criteria

1. Register an association of SHG's in society registration act, at district level.
2. Ensure financial self sufficient of the groups and to the society to carry out its mission at independent capacity.

Phase out strategies

1. Group meets at least 80% of the indicators of successful group development at group workshop.
2. Groups are restructured to a membership of 15-20.
3. Sankul is restructured at Panchayat level.
4. At least 80% groups are becoming saving groups and practicing internal lending.
5. Each group has its basic Constitution documented with crystal clear goal. Groups have an

understanding of local issues and are able to relate them with their actions.

6. SHG actively participate in village development activities, other than Mahila Samakhya.

Phase out indicators

1. Above 80% savings fund is rotated in lending activity and 95% repayments recorded.
2. Group maintains/arrange to maintain its accounts, minute registers and records independently.
3. Sakhies are active and take initiatives in facilitating group activities without external support.
4. Sahyoginis role in transferred.
5. Group conflicts are resolved by arbitration within village.

The Federation of Mahila Samooh has been formed in Rohtas as well as Muzaffarpur district for the sustainability of the Mahila Samakhya programme. District and State level workshops were organized for this purpose. Federation of groups has already been registered in Rohtas district while it is in the process of registration in Muzaffarpur district. The Federation of Rohtas submitted a project proposal to Bihar Education Project Council, Patna.

Overview

Mahila Samakhya in Bihar operates as a part of the Bihar Education Project. It was felt that the efforts at women's empowerment will be sustainable only when the gains accruing from primary education were available to all women. Without this, the efforts in all other sectors for women's amelioration will come to naught. The Mahila Samakhya programme is basically a revolutionary education programme for women, empowering them to take informed, responsible decision and leadership in the positive reshaping of family and society. In Mahila Samakhya, the educational process and methodology is based on respect for women's existing knowledge, experience and skill .

Mahila Samakhya has played an important role in the development and empowerment of women of Rohtas and Muzaffarpur districts in Bihar. Formation of women groups, saving groups and their Federation are the remarkable achievement of this programme. Education, training, awareness generation are the important programmes for the development of adolescent girls and women in both the districts. The impact of these programmes is felt in the development of positive attitude towards education, health, hygiene and sanitation at personal as well as village level. The activities of saving groups created zeal for entrepreneurship among rural women. It has awakened the potentialities and skills of women Mahila Shikshan Kendra played a great role in capacity building among 15 - 35 age group of adolescent girls and women. It urges rural girls and women to join the mainstream of development.

In the beginning, it was the Sahyoginis or the District Mahila Samakhya Core Team which took the intiative of mobilizing the women around various issues. But now that the Samoohs are aware of their strength and have build up their confidence, they have started talking issues concerning their social deprivation, by themselves. It is only when outside intervention becomes absolutely necessary, that they approach the higher authorities. Some of the major issues raised by the Mahila samoohs are concerned with land based issues struggle for minimum wages and equal wages; protest against alcoholism, child marriage, emolument and retention of girl children in schools, literacy of women and adolescent girls; construction of approach roads and wells in villages, gender issues, dowry deaths and many others.

The Mahila samoohs play a pivotal role in enrolment of children in the primary schools. The Mahila samooh on its part is responsible for the enrolment of the children from the villages. Throughout the district the Mahila samoohs organize enrolment rallies. The role of the samooh does not end with the enrolment of children and the distribution of text books to primary schools. The samoohs are also entrusted with the task of the constant monitoring of the schools with a view to reduce the drop-out rates. This also keeps the teachers alert and regular. Programmes like Jagjagi Kendras, literacy camp and Mahila Shikshan Kendras, the Mahila Samakhya caters to the education needs of the women and young girls.

The biggest change is to be seen in the attitude of the parents/guardians. The mothers, especially, who were vehemently opposed to the education of their girls are today sending their girls to school regularly. This change is especially noticeable in villages where the Mahila Samakhya has been actively advocating for the education of the girl child.

Although many types of training are being imparted to the women but for the economic empowerment there is demand for entrepreneurship development training programme for the women. Women groups have not been trained for productive purposes at village level. There is poor backward and forward linkages of groups.

The main difficulty in the smooth functioning of Mhila Samakhya is shortage of staff. It has caused a lot of confusion among the members of Mahila samooh and Bachat samooh. Musahar women were not associated with Bachat samooh in Rohtas. At the time of meeting for the discussion about Mahila samooh they did not mix with other women of the same village. Networking with the other government department was also lacking. Mahila samooh requires more training for production, marketing of goods and creation of self employment in the village itself.

These six years of Mahila Samakhya in Rohtas have really managed to bring out a palpable change in the society. Not only are the women more aware and forthcoming, but have also developed the confidence to tackle issues concerning their lives, by themselves. The most concipicuous achievement of Mahila Samakhya may be seen in the support that the programme has managed to elicit from the men, inspite of the initial antagonism. The impact on education, especially with concern for the girl child, is another appreciable effect

A. Status of Mahila Samakhya

	Districts							
	Rohtas	**W. Chmparan**	**Muzaffarpur**	**Sitamrhi**	**Darbhanga**	**Bhojpur**	**Gaya**	**Total**
Block covered	4	5	5	13	2	2	3	34
Panchayat covered	53	125	105	90	49	33	29	484
Village covered	357	330	410	300	250	189	228	2064
Sahyoginis	28	30	32	29	21	14	21	175
Trained Sakhis	711	964	1124	745	434	200	533	4711
Mahila Samooh	370	470	572	380	240	252	353	2637
No. of Women in Smooh	11986	10805	13308	7693	4573	4367	7499	60231
Trained samooh	272	234	282	261	113	122	128	1412
Samooh mainta-ining thrift credit	404	322	504	365	202	108	286	2191
Likages								
SGSY	24	15	212	37	10	0	0	298
NABARD	13	54	33	56	0	0	4	160
Total enrolment village	111	49	54	10	10	20	65	319

B. Status of Mahila Samakhya

	Districts							
	Rohtas	W. Chmparan	Muzaffarpur	Sitamrhi	Darbhanga	Bhojpur	Gaya	Total
Jagjagi centre	89	136	259	290	170	215	61	1220
Women in Jagjagi enrolled	1270	593	1117	968	202	836	451	5437
Girls enrolled in jagjagi	1547	3300	7305	6130	3649	1264	2013	25208
Bal Jagjagi centres	40	120	151	120	50	80	52	613
Girls enrolled in Bal	707	2909	2549	2583	1205	1378	1068	12399
Jagjagi Boys enrolled in Bael Jagjagi	638	1591	2448	1717	510	970	930	8804
Kishoris Manch	127	84	137	90	86	94	73	691
Girls in Manch	3309	1644	2438	2047	2237	2576	1961	16212
Trained Kishoris	727	630	944	916	326	293	337	4173
M.S. K. No.of Mobile Libraries	1 28	1 6	1 31	1 8	0 7	0 6	1 57	6* 143
Trained women Mason.	10	16	36	24	6	14	32	138

•* (5+1=6) One MSK is located in a non-MS district; Sheikhpura run by an NGO.

Source : Bihar Education Project Council, Patna.

of the programme. Not only more are girls attending the primary schools, but the drop out rates too, has been significantly reduced. Through its Kihsori Manch and Mahila Shikshan Kendras, M. S. has managed to give a new outlook in life to the adolescent girls and young women. Its savings and credit programme has also given an impetus to savings and micro credit enterprises among women.

Efforts of Mahila Samakhya are laudable but it has miles to go. This programme has to be extended in other blocks of Rohtas and Muzaffarpur districts so that more and more women are covered by it.

References

Needs India (1999): The Dawn of a New Beginning, Mahila Samakhya, Needs-India, Deoghar.

Ramchandran, Vimala (2002) : Education and the Status of Women; India Education Report, A Profile of Basic Education edited by R. Govinda, National Institute of Educational Planning and Administration. pp - 251-264.

Sachchidananda (2003): Empowerment of Scheduled Caste Women in Bihar, Sponsored by Ministry of Social Justice and Empowerment, Govt. of India, New Delhi, Conducted by Sulabh Institute of Development Studies, Patna.

The Mahila Samakhya Initiative (1999) : UNICEF, Patna.

9

SCHEDULED CASTE RESIDENTIAL SCHOOLS : A Case Study

RAJ KUMAR PANDEY

Any effort towards realizing the constitutional commitment of universal education for all children must seriously address the constraints that have hitherto excluded large sections of Indian society from education. Among the educationally most deprived sections in India are the Scheduled Castes. Scheduled Castes account for 14.71% of the population of Bihar. Only 19.31% of them were literate. Among the women the percentage was as low as 7.33.

They have suffered centuries of social, economic and educational deprivation, specific provisions were incorporated to protect these communities from discrimination as well as to facilitate their development. Where education is concerned the Constitution directs the States to promote with special care the educational and economic interest of the Scheduled Castes (Article 46).

Despite a rigorous effort by the government at different level to improve the educational level of the Scheduled Caste children, the situation has not changed to the desired level. The progress of schooling among Scheduled Castes children has been relatively poor compared to that of the general population. Disparities in education within Scheduled Caste communities is again significant.

Most of these Scheduled Caste children are first generation learners. For their retention and proper education the school environment plays and important role. Whether the issue of adequate infrastructure or teacher-student ratio, situation is becoming worse day by day.

The present study will highlight status of Scheduled Castes residential schools in Bihar. The present study was conducted in two boys residential high schools and two girls residential high schools in Muzaffarpur and Nalanda districts. The boys residential school was situated at Pokhraira, about 20 km west of the district headquarter in Saraiya block and girls residential school was situated at Rajwara which in fact is a girl's high school located 15 km east of the district headquarter. This school is located in Musahari block of Muzaffarpur district. Both the boys and girls residential high schools of Nalanda district was situated in one campus at Rajgir.

The girl's school at Rajwara was started in1993. Construction work of the school started in the year 1990 and prior to that the school was located in a rented house in Ramdayalu Nagar area of Muzaffarpur town. Pokhriara Boy's school started functioning in the year 1960. This school is among the few schools which were started in the early phase of this programme. Residential girls high school Rajgir is run in the campus of residential boys high school near SDO office at Rajgir. Previously it was boy's school but during 1991 girl's school was opened in the same school. Although building for the residential school has already been constructed in Harnout but due to some reasons, the school has not been shifted. Hostel for the girls students is separate but classes are held together.

Every year in the month of November, the Deputy Director Welfare issues an advertisement for admission in these schools at the district level. The entry in these high schools are at two levels. One is at Class I and the other at Class VI. For entrance at Class I level there is only an oral test where as for admission in Class VI, a written test followed by an interview is conducted at the district level for all the schools. Principal from one school examines the ability of the student of another school in the interview. The guardians who want their ward admitted in these schools are supposed to indicate the school of their own choice for both the classes. Seats are limited and therefore, many guardians use pressure tactics to get their ward admitted. This includes getting letter of recommendation from M.L.A., M.P. and ministers. No fees is charged from the students.

Infrastructure

Infrastructure is the backbone of any institution. Many previous researches in field of education have earlier confirmed that an institution without proper infrastructure has failed to retain and educate students properly. Moreover on some occasions it has also discouraged the guardians to send their children in that school. For a boarding school, this issue becomes more urgent from both the angles. The school at Rajwara had a slight edge over the other school in terms of available infrastructure. At Rajwara, there was lack of adequate number of classrooms and therefore, Class I to III students were conducted in one room, resulting in multigrade teaching without a trained teacher for that. Otherwise physical condition of the class rooms was not poor. About 50 students out of 248 do not get benches. School has electricity but power is available only between 10.0 p.m. to 7.0 a.m. There is no generator and sometimes when there is load shedding, the students have to depend on kerosene lamp. For water supply, 5 hand pumps are available in the campus out of which only 3 are functional. There is an electric-motor pump along with a water tank in the campus to store water. Toilets are functional but are not in adequate for 248 girls. There is a well managed play ground in the middle of the school campus. Some sports apparatus was also available for the students. One corner of the Principal's chamber used as library with some books. Every year the school receives a grant of Rs. 2000/- to purchase books but the condition of couple of almirahs do not substantiate it. The collection of the books in the library and its position clearly reveals that it had no proper user.

The school at Pokhraira had separate class room for each class. But its maintenance is very poor. The condition of doors, windows, ceiling and blackboard is deplorable. Only three benches are available in the school with a total strength of 241 boys. There is no alternate arrangement, and therefore, the students have to sit on the floor, even in the higher classes. Teachers said that they have removed those three benches so that students do not fight for sitting on them. Even chairs and tables for teachers were not available in required number. Only one globe and few charts were available as teaching learning material (TLM). School has no electricity from several years. There are five hand pumps in the campus out of which only three are in operation. Out of these three, one is not in a position to pump potable water. The electric water motor of the school has been stored in a room due to absence of electricity and fear of theft. Most of the toilets are non functional and require repair. The library of the school is not located in a separate room and proper almirah to store books, even though the number of the books is large. The school has no collection of sports kit. Similarly the huge play-ground, situated in the centre of the school campus is in bad shape. The condition of the laboratory was not satisfactory. Supply of equipment in the laboratory is not regular.

The building of SC boys residential high school Rajgir

is designed for only one school but girls residential school is also run in the same building. Students from boys and girls high school sit in a single building. Their classes are held combined in each room. The physical condition of the class rooms is not good. There were no doors in five rooms. Windows in six rooms were broken. Some rooms had window frames without glass panes. There is no dining hall as well as kitchen in the school. Meal is prepared in the corridor. There are 20 broken toilets without water facility. There is lack of chair, table and telephone in the school. There is acute shortage of maps, chart and globe in the school. Only chalk and blackboards are available in the school. Library is located in only one almirah. Many books are kept on the floor. There is shortage of bench and desk for all the students. There are no benches and desks upto class VIth consequently students sit on the floor.

In the residential girls high school Rajgir there is inadequate facility for all the girls in the hostel. Due to shortage of bed 50 girls used to sleep on the floor. There is shortage of toilet also. What ever toilet is built in the hostel there are no stairs in the toilet. Consequently small girls are unable to use the toilets. Due to bad condition of drainage waste water does not flow properly. There was no proper wiring for electricity. Even telephone was not working due to lack of allotment for the payment of bill. There is no place for the library. There is no allotment for sports material for the students. Recreational and extra curricular activities have been neglected due to lack of fund.

The student strength from Class I to X of the academic year 2002 of the Rajwara girls school reveals that out of the total of 248 students, 80 students were of Chamar caste, followed by 70 Dusadh students, 29 tribal students, 25 Mushar students, 20 Dhobi students, 12 Mehtar students, 11 Pasi students and 1 student from Dom caste. It is essential to mention here that in both the schools, tribal students mainly belonging to

Oraon tribe of West Champaran were also enrolled. From the last three years their entry in these schools have been stopped after a letter to this effect was issued by the office of Director Welfare asking them to get enroll in schools especially meant for them. But those who were admitted three years back continue their studies. About 35% students of the total strength were present in the school at the time of my visit. The reason behind this low turn out may be that the teaching work of the school was suspended due to severe cold.

Pokhraira school reveals that in the academic year 2002 only 45 students were enrolled in Class II, out of which 18 students were from Dusadh caste followed by 17 Chamar, 8 Musahar and 1 student each from Dhobi and Pasi caste respectively. At class X level in the same year only 24 students were enrolled, out of which the tribal students were in maximum strength (17) about 15% were present in the school on the day of our visit.

Table 1 : Caste and school class-wise students in the Residential Girls school Rajgir during 2001

Caste / School Class	Musahar	Dome	Mehtar	Chamar	Dusadh	Dhobi	Rajbar	Dharhi	Pasi	Total
I	07	02	-	03	05	-	08	-	04	29
II	18	02	-	05	07	-	05	01	01	29
III	06	-	-	03	02	-	01	-	-	12
IV	06	-	-	03	01	-	01	-	-	11
V	04	-	-	06	01	-	-	-	-	11
VI	04	-	-	02	01	01	02	-	01	11
VII	03	-	-	06	02	-	06	-	03	20
VIII	10	-	-	06	02	-	03	-	02	23
IX	04	-	-	04	03	-	01	-	01	13
X	05	-	-	11	03	-	02	-	-	21
G. Total	67	04	-	49	27	01	29	01	12	190

The enrolment data for current year was not available There was no Mehtar girl student enrolled in the school. One girl student belonged to Dhobi and one to Dharhi castes were enrolled. Altogether four Dom girl students was enrolled in the school. The majority of the girl students belonged to Musahar, Mochi, Dusadh, Rajbar and Pasi castes. Mehtar, Dhobi, Darhi and Dom castes were lacking awareness for the enrolment in the residential school. Dom girl student belonged to Class I and II while Darhi girl student belonged to Class II but there was one Dhobi girl student in Class VI. Although 25% seats are reserved for the scavengers there is no enrolment of Mehtar girl student in any of the classes.

In SC boys residential school Rajgir, 248 students were enrolled. Hardly 1% boys belonged to Dom caste. There was lowest enrolment of children from Dom caste and dropout is high due to home environment. Due to

Table 2 : Caste and school class-wise enrolment in boy's School Rajgir

Caste / School Class	Nehtar	Dome	Musahar	Chamar	Dusadh	Rajbar	Pasi	Dhobi	Total
I									*5
II	6	-	13	7	4	4	5	1	41
III	1	-	8	5	6	5	2	1	28
IV	3	-	6	3	3	2	1	1	19
V	-	1	6	1	3	1	-	-	12
VI	-	-	4	1	2	-	-	-	7
VII	-	-	7	4	3	4	2	-	20
VIII	-	-	14	3	4	4	5	1	31
IX	-	-	13	3	4	4	6	-	30
X	-	1	13	6	4	3	6	-	33
Examinee (Matriculation)	-	-	8	3	3	2	6	-	22
G.Total	10	2	92	36	36	29	33	4	248

life style and food habit Dom children do not wait to continue their education. Dhobi and Mehtar boys enrolment was poor than other Scheduled castes. No mehtar caste student was studying beyond IVth class in the school. There was same case with Dhobi caste student, there was only one student of Dhobi caste belonged to Class VIII. The maximum number of enrolled students belonged to Musahar caste followed by Chamar, Dusadh, Pasi and Rajbar castes.

Teacher strength and their problems

At Rajwara girls high school the total number of sanctioned posts is 13 including Principal. At the time of study only 8 teachers including Principal were in position out of that, 2 teachers were on deputation. Under these circumstances the teacher-student ratio comes to 41.33. Although the ratio can not be said to be poor on the basis of national norm but absence of teachers from their total strength do have major implications. One of them is that the students do not get required specialist teacher for each subject, especially in higher classes. Another important aspect is that in a school where teaching of classes from I to X is conducted, it becomes impossible for 6 teachers to conduct all 10 classes simultaneously. This situation leads to multigrade teaching at different levels.

The teacher - student ratio of Pokharaira boys school is 26.77. It is because the number of sanctioned post is 17 including Principal, in which only 11 teachers including the Principal is posted there and again out of this strength, 2 teachers were suspended. Although the teacher - student ratio of the school seems to be healthy but one should not forget that in schools like this atleast one teacher per class is essential. Calculation by ratio is not going to help the school get out of multigrade teaching without specialized manpower.

There are only 5 teachers in the school against the sanctioned post of 11. There are only two teachers for high school while three for middle school. The teacher

- student ratio is 39. Subject wise teacher is not available in the school. Residential facilities are not given to the teacher. Teachers reported that there was inferiority complex among the teacher due to discrimination in retirement of age which is 58. There is no post of Hostel Superintendent in the school. Teachers are overburdened due to Mess work. Teachers do not perform their duties well due to extra curricular work. Teachers suggested that they should be spared from the mess work.

Against the sanctioned strength of 17 only 10 teachers at present in the residential boys schools at Rajgir in Nalanda district. There was one headmaster in the school. There were four teachers against post of 7 in the middle section while 5 against 9 for high section. There was no teacher for Geography, Economics and Hindi. There was one clerk in the school but he was on deputation at District Welfare Officer.

Teachers complained that no residential facilities is given to the teachers. Moreover, there was irregular payment of salary to the teachers. Teachers were given supervision of Messwork which creates tension between students and teachers in the school.

Extent of Drop-outs

Drop-out has always remained a crucial issue for education planners. Reason behind this is that in Bihar alone the drop out rate in the year 1998-99 for Class I to VIII was 66.34% (Source U.P.B.E.P.). But beyond expectation in these schools where the study was conducted, this acute problem which is manifested in almost every formal school was only symbolic. The girl's high school reported no drop out case in the last two years where as only 7 boys left school in high school Pokhariara during the same duration. One such boy was Sudhir Kumar Paswan who has reportedly went to Delhi to drive a lorry. Another boy is Amit Kumar who left the school to join another school for getting better education.

Student problems

The condition of hostels in both the schools is deplorable from every angle. Neither there are adequate rooms for all the students to live nor does the hostel have required furniture. Only 100 beds are available for 248 girls. In the boy's school 166 more beds are needed to meet the total requirement. In both the schools the number of cooks is less than the sanctioned posts. In the girl's high school 2 male cook are working, although the post is meant for female staff. In the boy's high school bulk of hostel rooms lacked doors and windows and the students have to suffer from hot or cold winds in different seasons.

Condition of toilets and bathrooms was very poor in the hostels. Similarly the mess is not in a condition to supply clean and hygienic food to its boarders. Quality of food served to the students was actually not verified, but in both the schools there was a food menu chart, based on which the food is served. Functional Common room and hostel and library do not exist.. Both these school hostels got a colour Television way back in early nineties but it stopped functioning after few years due to lack of power and maintenance.

The condition of boys and girls high school Rajgir was also bad. There was no arrangement of beds for sleeping. There is no allotment for the sport and game. Students arrange for sports spending their own money. They came from poorest section of the society. Poor guardians are unable to spend money for the sports and game. There is need to arrange sports material for the student and there must be allotment for the same. Books are not supplied in time so student feel difficulty for want of books. There was no bench and desk for the students upto class VIth. There is no proper arrangement of seating in the class room and beds in the hostel. There was acute shortage of teaching learning materials in the school.

Pattern of financial support to the school

The School receives financial allotment under two broad categories. One is for salary and the other for school maintenance. Usually now a days the schools are receiving their grant delayed by four to six months. This makes the condition of food supplier miserable. The teachers also find it hard to cope with the situation. Rs. 500/- per month per boy is given to the school for the meal and breakfast. Rs. 20 per boy is given for oil, soap and cleaning material which is inadequate for bathing and washing. Rs. 500 per year per boy is given for two sets of shirt pant. Similarly Rs. 50 per boy per annum is given for the medical facilities and Rs. 400 for Teaching learning material is given per boy per annum. Allotment is given during September and October. This is why the condition upto March becomes congenial but during April to August the problem is always acute. There is no allotment for the game, electricity, and telephone etc. Books and answer books are supplied but it takes long to materialise as there are hurdles at many stages.

Teachers reported even at the end of January, books have not been supplied. Answer books have already supplied to the students. During last year, books were supplied in the months of March and April.

School Inspection

School inspection is shoddy. Frequency of visits by the inspecting authorities is very few on records. The boy's high school was visited by the Chairman of Zila Parishad, the District Magistrate and others officers. However, most of the inspection conducted is internal and has nothing to do with the progress of the school.

In recent years due to formation of different bodies under local self government, the members of Zila Parishad have also started inspecting these schools but their main intention is to make some political mileage.

Similarly from time to time local MLA also arrange meetings in these schools but the school never gains from such meetings.

It is customary for these schools to offer hospitality for the guests who make a visits. But situation becomes untolerable when an uncalled person makes a call. It is reported by the school authorities of the Pokhariara boy's high school that they usually have to pay money to local extortionist on the pretext of a festival. This is met by contribution from all the staff. The teachers fear that refusal can create an unnecessary tussle. This matter has been reported to the District Welfare Officer several times but in vain.

Departmental inspecting officers never ask about teaching learning environment, result and performance of the students. They only ask about only meal. DWO, Deputy Director, Director Welfare are the inspecting officers from Department. Non-departmental officials are DM, DDC, and DEO etc.

Parent - Teacher Association (PTA)

There is no Parent - Teacher Association (PTA) in these schools. But occasionally the school administration invites parents in school to discuss issues related with their children's education. Certain functions are organized not more than two times in a year. In Pokharaira school there is a school monitoring committee in which there are five members. Two members are from Scheduled caste community and the rest are selected from local social workers irrespective of their caste. This monitoring committee meets eight to ten times a year and makes some suggestions for improving the situation.

Performance level of students

So far as the performance level of the students of these schools are concerned it is outstanding at board level exam. About 85% students passed the board exam from Pokhraira school in 2001. This figure fall to 59%

in the year 2002. In the girl's high school Rajwara about 90% students passed in the 2001 Board examination. This figure dropped to 55% in 2002.

Overview and suggestions

(a) From any standard the existing condition of the school building, number of required room for teaching and stay, condition of toilets and bathrooms and overall infrastructure is not adequate. The schools are languishing. Government should intervene immediately so that the shape of these schools gets changed. The New Education Policy (1986) has promised a conducive environment for learning along with proper education.

(b) Children who are overaged also get admitted in these schools. Many of them in higher classes become rowdies. There should be some mechanism to check over age students entering in the two entry level classes. Similarly inter-district admission method should be adopted. This will not only insulate the administration from the outside pressure which they face at the time of admission but will also restrict the students from visiting their home frequently.

(c) One of the basic purposes of setting up of residential schools was to address the educational problem of people who are most deprived among the deprived communities. This purpose has failed as children from better off families are admitted and restrict the chance for others. Sometimes two or more children from same family got enrolled. It is high time to make some modifications in the admission procedure so that not more than one child from a·family get the benefit of studying in these schools. Annual family income and guardian's profession should also be considered at the time of admissions.

(d) The funds allotted for medical expenses of the

students is meager. It can be overcome if the doctor posted at nearest block is asked to make atleast one visit in a week to check the health of the students. It is more important in the girl's high school which has more closed atmosphere. This will also relieve the school administration from paying the consultancy fees to the doctor.

(e) There is need to make quarters for teachers so that the school may be completely residential. This will enable the teachers to provide more time to students and will change the school environment.

(f) Performance of all students are not equal, obviously due to their different back-ground. It is necessary to run remedial classes for the mediocre students to improve their performance as well as to sustain their interest in their studies.

(g) At present these schools are isolated. Strong linkages should be established between SC communities and school through parent - teachers association, Village Education Committees, etc, to mobilize SC communities to take greater advantage of educational facilities provided, by the government. Study tour of SC students may also be encouraged so that awareness of what is happening around may be created amongst them.

(h) In the educational institutions like this the atmosphere may be made conducive for the participation of the parents of the SC children by organizing functions, exhibitions etc. Thus the linkage can be established. Further the students may be allowed to participate in the development programmes in the area during summer vacations / holidays so that they can earn and learn. This would also instil a sense of awareness in them about the various development programmes implemented for them. Emphasis may be laid for imparting vocational training in technical education, training in agriculture, horticulture, etc, to the students in the school after the classes so that they would be able to earn their livelihood in future.

(i) Although teachers in these schools are well educated but they do not have in service training. We always witness instant changes in teaching method, pedagogy, Teaching Learning Material (TLM), etc, coming out from time to time. Therefore it is essential that the teachers of these schools should be made aware about these through organizing orientation camps.

(j) These schools should have N.C.C.. This will not only keep the students engaged but will also develop a sense of patriotism among them.

(k) Like other government departments, release of funds are delayed for several months in these schools. This creates problems for the school. There is an urgent need to improve the situation so that things run smoothly.

(l) The quality of answers books, stationary, dress and blanket provided to the students should be improved. At present the quality of supplied items is poor.

(m) Efforts should be made to make academic inspections of these school. Usually inspection does not probe about teaching in these schools.

(n) With a view to bring some radical change these schools could be handed over to reputed N.G.Os with unimpeachable credentials as has been done in Gujarat. We can hope, this might prove beneficial for the students for whom the school has been established.

(o) Vacancy of teachers should be filled up so that there should not be any shortage of teacher for a particular subject. Teachers should not be engaged in the Mess management . There must be provision for water and toilet in the schools.

(p) There is need to provide infrastructural facilities and to construct more rooms and repair of building.

(q) Environment building programme is needed for the enrolment and retention of Mehtar and Dom children particularly girl children in the school. DWO and BWO should help the teachers in the solution of problems at the school level. They should look into the academic problems of the school but they do not do so.

(r) There should be medical examination of children before getting admission in the school otherwise many problems crop up afterwards as reported by the teacher.

(s) There should be teachers-guardian coordination committee in the school so that both can be aware of the problem of the students. This will enable teachers to convince guardians for the enrolment and retention of the students in the school particularly girl student. There is lack of awareness among guardians of the scheduled caste children. Majority of them do not know the facilities given by Government for the educational development of the SC children.

(t) There must be separate arrangement of teaching and accommodation for the girl students in the girls high school Rajgir. They should not be in the same campus. There must be Superintendent's quarter in the school so that both the hostels should be supervised and controlled by him. There is none to look after the boys hostel at night. Teachers quarters should be made inside the campus.

References

Deliege, Robert (1999) : The Untouchables of India, Oxford Univesity Press, New Delhi.

Department of Education (1986) : National Policy on Education 1986, Ministry of Human Resource Development, Government of India, New delhi.

Kumar, N. (2003) : Schedule Caste Residential Schools : A Case Study of Muzaffarpur District, (Unpublished Report), Sulabh Institute of Development Studies, Patna.

Pandey, Raj Kumar (2003) : Scheduled Caste Residential Schools : A Case Study of Nalanda District, (Unpublished Report), Sulabh Institute of Development Studies, Patna.

10

LITERACY AND DEVELOPMENT

SACHCHIDANANDA

Soon after the new countries of the third world threw off the colonial yoke, they addressed themselves to the task of development. They had to catch up with the advanced countries of the West in the shortest possible time. For some time, there was the controversy whether economic development or education should be given the highest priority. The question was to provide certain economic base as it was assumed that only if increased production income is available does good education become possible. However, with the passage of time, it came to be realized that development could only be meaningful and sustained if people were educated. Education is an important aspect of level of living for fuller life. In poor countries it has definite effect on human productivity and constitutes an important form of investment. It is highly complex concept open to many different interpretations.

Development requires more than education. It involves institutional change in attitude of people. It also requires modernization of the socioeconomic structure. Without literacy farmers will not be able to improve their understanding of the importance and the implications of development or to affect the technical knowledge necessary for economic growth. Literacy through adult education allows full scope for creative imagination and innovation. Its aim is to achieve more efficient and just society. Literacy has an important role in reducing inequalities in growth. The explanation of inequalities is to be found in internal structure and behaviour pattern, available resources, population, socioeconomic system, methods of production, mental outlook, culture and educational system. There is a positive correlation between level of training and information and growth levels.

The prerequisite for education as an instrument of social change, is the relative independence of the education system from political authorities and a guarantee of freedom of expression for teachers and pupils.

Literacy and Development before NAEP

In India, the importance of literacy through adult education was realized as early as 1928, by the Royal Commission on Agriculture. The report of the Commission emphasizes the role of literacy in the following words :

> "It is clear that while a universal system of rural education for children is obviously indispensable for the future, it cannot affect the present situation and if it is not to be supplemented by a determined effort to spread adult education, many of the improvements in agriculture which we so earnestly desire to see, must be postponed until a new generation has sprung up fitted by early tuition to reap the advantages we are seeking to place within their reach. That appreciable progress has been achieved in popularizing the idea of adult education indicates that the people are willing to accept new opportunities and to depart from old custom. The very fact that adult schools have been started is evidence that some adults have been convinced that it is worth their while to attend. It may be that disappointments have been great and failures many, but it is encouraging that efforts have been made, have been responded to and

have even met some measure of success."

"We are much attracted by the possibility which a development of adult education at a large scale holds out. Such a development would antedate by at least a generation that great advance in literacy, which, in our view, is essential to progress in all directions. Its influence in enlarging the scope of the cultivator's horizon and in increasing his willingness to adopt agricultural improvements and his capacity to watch over its own interest in buying and selling commodities and products would be immense. Even more important is the stimulus which would be given to the spread of primary education amongst the youth of both sexes. A great obstacle to educational advance is presented by the apathy of the parents and no better method of overcoming this can be devised, than by inducing them to realize in their own persons the benefits of education. What may be described as the aftercare of the literacy won at the primary school stage will be immensely facilitated, for the spread of literacy among the parents will create a demand for the supply of the printed matter which is still seldom met within rural districts in India and will thus give to the village libraries which now require fostering care from educational and other official authorities, the secure basis of popular support."

Illiteracy presents the most formidable, single obstacle to rural development in the widest sense.

In its recommendations the Commission included the following :

(1) Spread of literacy among the women of India is of great importance for rural development.

(2) The influence of female education in spreading lasting literacy among the young should be ascertained with a view to demonstrating the true relation between female literacy and the spread of general literacy.

(3) The advancement of adult education is a matter of own official activity rather than for the Government Department, but the latter who assist it in all possible ways.

The report of the Ancillary Committee of Indian Statutory Commission, 1929, which was headed by Sir Philip Hartog, highlighted the importance and role of literacy for the political education of Indians. The Commission realized that education is not an indispensable requisite for an intelligent exercise of the vote. Many people unable to read or write are capable of knowing clearly within narrow range of their experience what they want and of making an intelligent selection of a representative from some of their literate fellow villagers. The Commission further noted :

> "But we need hardly labour to establish the proposition that education does help in the formation of an electorate which will be potentially more capable of understanding issues submitted to its judgement and hence prima facie better equipped to exercise political power. We are justified, therefore, in regarding the extent of popular education as a not untrustworthy general guide to people's fitness for the exercise of political privileges and the prevalence of literacy is the commonest and the most easily ascertainable index to the stage reached in mass education. True, literacy alone affords no guarantee of the attainment of real political capacity but the ability to read at least increases the probability that statements and discussion of political issues and political programmes will reach the electors. It simplifies also the essential mechanics of the polling booth, for it means or ought to mean that the voter will be able to cast his vote in the proper ballot box without the aid of colour or symbol or of some more questionable guidance."

The Committee on emotional integration set up under the chairmanship of Dr. Sampurnanand in the early sixties highlights the need for evolving an adult education programme linked with the occupational interest and the cultural background of the people. In its report it stressed the following :

> "Next to technical and primary education very high priority should be accorded to Adult Education Programme in view of their importance in the circumstance prevailing in the country today. It is ultimately the economic development of the people that goes to promote national integration and one of the biggest obstacles in bringing about such a development rapidly is the alarming extent of illiteracy in our country."

Any organized system of adult education should, therefore, ensure that men and women, in addition to acquiring vocational and teaching skills, are given a general education which will foster in them a sense of abiding values of the faculty of critical judgement. To discount prejudice and to arrive at a balanced view in all matters should be one of the first lessons taught in the Adult Education Programme.

The majority of the adult population work in the agricultural sector and the adult farmers must be educated to make use of the best extension methods available to raise their standard of living and to contribute their best to national wealth. It is also necessary to organize some suitable programme to give them the necessary education in the acquisition of certain simple skills and certain type of work which can be done at home during their spare time.

In 1967, a committee of members of Parliament was appointed to prepare a draft statement of the National Policy on Education in the light of the recommendations of the Kothari Commission. The committee made its recommendation as follows:

> "The liquidation of mass illiteracy is essential not only for accelerating programmes of production specially in agriculture but for quickening the tempo of national development in general. Plans

to accelerate the spread of literacy should, therefore, be prepared and intensively implemented in several parts. With a view to reducing new additions to the ranks of adult illiterates, part-time literacy classes should be organized for grown up children (age-group 11-17) who did not attend schools and have lapsed back into illiteracy. All employees in large commercial, industrial and other concerns should be made functionally literate within a prescribed period of their employment and a lead in this direction should be given by the industrial plants in the public sector. Similarly teachers, students and educational institutions should be actively involved in literacy campaign, especially as a part of the social or national services programme. The achievement of literacy should be sustained by the provision of attractive written material and library services to the new literates."

Literacy and the NPE

The National Policy of Education envisages that adult education would be a means of reducing economic, social and other disparities, and the nation, as a whole, will assume the responsibility for providing the resource support for implementing programmes for educational transformation, reducing disparities, universalization of elementary education, adult literacy etc. The removal of women's illiteracy and obstacles inhibiting their access to and retention in elementary education will receive overriding priority through a provision of special support services. Adult education would also support the process of liberation from ignorance and oppression. The critical development issue today is the continuous upgradation of skills so as to produce manpower resources of the kind and the number required by society. Since participation by beneficiaries in the development programmes is of crucial importance, systematic programmes of adult education, linked with national goals such as alleviation of poverty, national integration, environmental conservation, the energization of cultural creativity of the people, observance of small family norm, promotion of women's equality etc. would be organized and the existing programme reviewed and strengthened.

Concept of Literacy

The concept of literacy is not equated with the mere ability to read and write. Literacy, if it is to be worthwhile, must be functional. It should enable the literate not only to acquire sufficient mastery on the tools of literacy, but also to acquire sufficient mastery of relevant knowledge which will enable him to pursue his own interests and ends. The literacy programmes should have three essential ingredients: (i) It must be, as far as possible, work-based and aimed at creating interest and imparting skills and information which will help a person to do efficiently whatever work he/she is engaged in; (ii) It must help the literate to interest himself/herself in vital national problems and to participate effectively in the social and political life of the country; (iii) It must impart such skills in reading, writing and arithmetic as it would enable his/her, if he/she so wishes, to continue hi /her education either on his/her own or through other available avenues off informal education.

It follows that literacy programmes will have three stages. The initial stage will consist of acquaintance with reading, writing and arithmetic with some general knowledge relating to civic and national problems in which the entire society is involved and to the profession in which the learner is engaged. The second stage should deepen the knowledge and skills gained in the initial stage and train the adult in using the literacy gained for solving personal problems and enriching personal life. The third stage should lead the adult to one of the programmes for continuing education.

Correlation between Literacy and certain Aspects of Development

Education is a prime factor in development. It is expected to improve productivity in all sectors of the economy including agriculture. A literate person is likely to adopt modern technology in agriculture. Literacy rate is associated with increased agricultural productivity. Baldeo Singh in his study arrived at a conclusion that the literacy of the decision-maker, as well as, agricultural worker has a positive correlation with productivity. In most of the studies a definite positive relationship is observed between literacy rates and agricultural productivity. Functional literacy is expected to affect the ability of the farmers in adopting modern inputs in agriculture. However, in most of the studies the correlates of literacy such as higher socioeconomic status, better exposures to outside influence, higher income and the ability to put in agriculture inputs at the right time have not been taken into consideration. Some researches carried out in Bihar in the late sixties revealed a positive relationship between literacy and the adoption of new practices in agriculture. It was found that in almost all the villages under study the literate peasants had a higher rate of adoption of innovations in agriculture in regard to new seeds, fertilizers, insecticides as well as agricultural implements. It was seen that the literate peasants received message about the innovations earlier than illiterate respondents.

An attempt was made to study the relationship between literacy rate and percentage of main workers to total population. The coefficient of correlation between these two appears to be significant. It is generally believed that literate farmers switch over to nonfood crops where the returns are assumed to be better. Hence, literacy rate is known to have positive relationship with the percentage area under nonfood crops. However, this does not hold true in all areas.

The correlation between education and population growth rates may be indicative of the educated being able to adopt modern family planning techniques and force down rising birth rate. Research has shown that mass education at primary level is far more effective in reducing family size than the education of the elite. Family welfare programmes seen to be more successful among literate than among the illiterate. It is believed that widespread literacy tends to reduce family size. The literate person tends to be receptive to new ideas, new practices propagated by change agents. P. R. Gopinathan Nair analysed the relationship between education and demographic variables. In a number of societies, the attainment of literacy brings with it a sharp decline in family size. Several studies show that as women acquire literacy, they reduce their number of children by roughly one-third.

Literacy and other levels of education have definite correlation with infant mortality. It is seen that both for India and Bihar, in rural and urban areas, the educational level of mothers has a direct bearing on infant mortality. The following table amply illustrates this. It is thus, clear that infant mortality rates can be effectively reduced if a higher percentage of women in the childbearing age are educated or at least made literate.

Estimate of children dying at the age of 5 per thousand live births in 1981 by educational levels of mothers

Educational levels	Rural	Urban
Educational level	178	126
Illiterate	119	64
Literate but below middle	83	60
Below matriculation	62	42
Below graduate	47	29
Graduate and above	-	-

Literacy and Women

Although it has been admitted that the impact of the adult education programme has been far from impressive, the winds of change have begun to blow in many areas. An evaluation of the impact of adult literacy on women's development was made in Gujarat in 1985. 114 respondents were examined to evaluate the impact of adult literacy on fertility and childcare. Although the sample was small, the results were significant. They are indicative of the beginning of change; it is clear that there have been some limited gains. The overall majority of the respondents have learnt about family planning. They were aware of sterilization. A higher percentage of awareness was found about vasectomy as compared to tubectomy. In the case of spacing method, their awareness was poor.

The impact of adult education on fertility in a short span is less easily discernible; its impact on childcare can be more easily seen. It is clear that mothers in adult education centres gave greater weightage to education of their children. However, they were more keen to send their boys to schools than the girls. This, of course, is in consonance with the situation prevailing in much of Indian countryside. One important aspect of childcare is that pertaining to health and hygiene. Some improvements were visible in this respect. Ninety-two percent of the mothers attending the adult education centres reported that they had all got their children vaccinated. Most of the women were also breast-feeding their infants. In times of ill health or illness, over 86 percent of the mothers reported that they would seek medical help. On the whole, literacy seems to have had some beneficial effect on the health and hygiene of children.

However, in the matter of their attitude and perception, it appears that even after attaining literacy, traditional beliefs and age-old myths still stick to a large percentage of women. This is borne out by the fact that quite a few women did not find anything wrong with dowry. They still entertain a favourable attitude towards it even though dowry has been legally banned. In the case of gender equality there were a number of women who willingly accepted the idea of a subservient position of women in the family. Some of them even asserted that husbands had more brains. Male superiority did not appear to them obnoxious. Subjugated in their personal life and sequestered in public life, there are many women in the lower rung of society who are still not aware of their basic rights, much less able to fight for them. They are often marginalized in the decision-making process in the family, society and the political system.

It is unrealistic to expect literacy by itself to produce spectacular changes in the lives of women in the prevailing socioeconomic situation of the rural India, characterized by want and privation on many fronts and veneration of age-old beliefs and practices which have tended to keep women in a state of semi-serfdom. Alongwith other activities such as providing employment opportunities, improving their living standard, creating a consciousness of their own rights and dignity etc., adult education is, however, a harbinger of women's development. Literacy has helped the learners in becoming self-confident and conscious. When an investigator asked one of the learners as to why he had been taking pains in attending the Adult Education Centre, the reply was : "You cannot know the utility. While cutting the earth we can make our own calculation and can very well see whether the amount we are paid has been correctly entered in the wage register. We also help our fellow workers who are not literate in calculating their wages." An air of confidence and pride is clearly visible when a new literate is narrating these gains flowing out from his newly acquired skill in literacy and numeracy.

Literacy and the Weaker Sections of the Population

"For the poor, education means food and clothing", Gandhiji said way back in 1943. By putting it in these words, he had meant that for education to be meaningful it must be correlated with the living and working conditions of the people. Functionality and awareness are but two aspects aimed at creating economic viability and awareness of the existing facilities. In a study made in Bihar it was revealed that the majority of the learners had been made aware of the facilities available from the Primary Health Centre and the Agricultural and Veterinary Centres. Information regarding the upgrading of their functionality was available to more than 80 percent of the respondents. This includes information regarding improved seeds, fertilizers and scientific agricultural techniques. Some material prepared by the Indian Council of Agricultural Research was passed on to agriculturists in simple language. This conveyed to them certain information regarding cropping patterns and improved variety of maize. In some centres, bank officials discussed with the learners the facilities provided by the banks. Similarly, the veterinary doctors talked to them about the problems of cattle.

At another place, it was found that by way of functional efficiency a number of neo-literates belonging to Scheduled caste community obtained cycles-rickshaws through the Bank of India. Some Musahars have started piggeries with the assistance of the Animal Husbandry Department. A number of Dusadhs, another Scheduled caste, have opened savings bank accounts in the bank. Charkhas have been given to women attending these centres through the Khadi and Village Industry Boards. The doctors and the paramedical staff, the bank managers, the District Development Officers and Agricultural Supervisors have periodically met village people and have informed them of the government's programmes for self-employment. Socioeconomic benefits of development, which had either not reached the weaker sections or communities, are reaching them now. Through cooperation, the neo-literates are moving towards self-reliance. Though such cases are not many, the trend is obvious. At many places, at the initiative of the learners, huts have been put up for the running of these centres. The cooperation of social workers has been described as positive. Purchase of mats, cleaning the centres etc., are steps in the total process of self reliance. A change in the attitude of the upper class people may be seen when we find upper class instructors teaching lower class learners and working for their cause. The learner feels satisfied. In some cases, women instructors, belonging to the Rajput caste have been running centres for the Scheduled castes. Thus, the barriers of the castes and class are crumbling.

Inhibitions among the women are giving way. They are coming up as instructors and learners. Women who were used to be behind the walls are now talking to strangers. Some women learners exclaimed that being literate, they now know how to talk to people outside.

There is ample evidence of newly literate raising their voice against injustice and exploitation. This is a constant source of trouble for the elite who fear that it would upset their long-standing monopoly of power. In one area of North Bihar every village where an Adult Education Centre exists, awareness groups *(chetna sanghas*) are organized as watchdogs against exploitation. This is a unified force of the people in the peaceful bulwark against injustice in villages. As the poor are organizing for a life with dignity, the vested interests would like the centres to be closed. This is evident because in some areas enthusiastic adult education workers have been implicated by the landlords and other vested interests in false cases.

The traditional concept of womanhood has been eroded. The adult education programme has a strange impact on upper class women learners. For years, they were treated as showpieces to beautify the homes. Now they consider themselves to be contributors in economic matters also. In one area, women belonging to the Rajput caste demanded vocational training as well as work. They, were conscious of their status in society. Since they could not work in the field, they were eager to take up light work like spinning, knitting, preparing paper, bari, etc. Many women learners have demanded charkhas and sewing machines to supplement their family income.

Although, the age group for the Adult Education Centre is 15 to 35, in many centres we find children below 15, as well as, people over 35 years. Children often accompanied their parents. Due to abject poverty, the children do not go to primary schools. Thus the Centres are serving as places for transgenerational education. In one Centre, the father and his little daughter were found studying together. The father was insisting on getting his daughter enrolled in one of the Centres. This shows how people are concerned about the education of their children. In many Centres little children were studying without being enrolled.

Literacy starts a continuous process, or say, a chain reaction. The learners are not the only beneficiaries from the Centres. When they organize protests against injustice, they include many more from the community. Thus, the knowledge of the learner percolates down to even those who are not enrolled at the Centres.

Literacy and the Tribals

The political assertion of economic rights and the accompanying process of the socialization of critical thought among the Adivasis, promises to create a social basis for the need of literacy. Some voluntary agencies working in the Thane district of Maharashtra have adopted literacy as a tool. They believe that the fundamental objective of all education is to encourage the people to posit an act of freedom. The awareness, which takes place in the process of people's education, that takes place continually, is also understood as an act of affirmation - the act of affirmation of confidence in oneself.

Hence, the awareness begins with the discovery of each person as a dignified human being. In the festivals, the 'self' image of individuals is built up. The image the people have of this is what determines their behaviour, and so a people acting for freedom must begin to regulate themselves as free human beings, people whom the bondage of poverty and deprivation, the marginalization and dehumanization will not crush. The awareness of the human person leads to the discovery of the other persons as well as, in the literacy camps. These agencies have organized their base upon the participatory approach. The thrust of literacy intervention is to provide inputs to raise the forces of production and confront the exploitative social relation, through collective social assertion to establish rights that are due to the people under the various development schemes of the government, to resist the extortion by the government officials, especially those of the police, revenue and forest department, to resist the alienation of Adivasi land to the landlords and traders, to address issues related to forests, State repression on women's question, anti-drunkenness drive, and finally, attempt to establish alternate forms of cooperative activity through committees to settle internal disputes.

All these actions are accompanied and followed by reflection in informal village groups, in meetings of the village committees, in those of coordination committees of the organization. It is through this process that awareness and enlightenment is being spread in the area. Voluntary effort in institutionalized education in the region is a more efficient instrument than that of the State in promising all-round development.

Literacy and Income -Generation Activities

In different parts of India, acquisition of literacy has been linked with development programmes. The RFLP project in Kurnool had achieved creditable success in linking literacy effort with the activities of development agencies in the district. In collaboration with the District Rural Development Agency, they have arranged for training of adult women learners in tailoring and plastic caning. The women in that Centre are striving hard to learn and also to earn at the same time and trying to

They are now able to keep accounts and calculate their wages. It has also helped them in bringing up their children properly. They have also become conscious of the need for family planning and limiting the size of their families. Their general knowledge about the people, places and their environment has increased very much. The villagers are now vocal about the absence of electricity and proper health facilities. They also want to undergo training in tailoring, soap making and such other useful activities so that they can raise their income.

In another village, in the same district, called Khambari, people are entirely dependent on forest produce for their livelihood. Most of them were engaged in cutting bamboo and preparing different types of baskets, containers, frames, mats, screens, decorative item etc. Before the Adult Education Centre was established there, the bamboo workers were selling their products at different rates. After the Centre was established, these workers have formed into a sort of a cooperative for the sale of their products. In fact, they have come to an understanding among themselves not to sell their products at lower rates. They have now fixed uniform prices for different articles. They are now able to make a decent living out of the sale of their products. This is the immediate tangible benefit of adult education in this area. The villagers are also found of be vocal about the demand for electricity and health centres.

The women learners want to learn new things. They are aware that bamboos may not last long in the forest. They want to switch over to preparing baskets and other things with plastic wires. They also want to learn the art of tailoring. There is a new sense of confidence and purpose among youth workers which should pave the way for their further development. Already, many families have crossed the poverty line with better income from bamboo articles. They are now aware of the need for education and want to send their children to school regularly. Women are also conscious about the need to limit their families.

Literacy has brought new life for many individuals. Taruni is a neo-literate from a village, five kilometres from Bolangir. Before she joined the adult education centre, she was very timid. Her husband, a woodcutter in the jungle, was addict to liquor and spent all his income on it. Taruni, being the mother of two children, had to face a lot of difficulties in running the family and bringing up the children. She had no land or property. All that she possessed in the world was a hut made of mud with thatched roof. After attending the Adult Education classes and coming into contact with other learners, Taruni started taking positive steps to improve her lot. With the help of the Adult Education instructors, she gradually persuaded her husband to give up drinking. Slowly and steadily, her effort bore fruit. Her husband stopped drinking. Gradually, she also started saving money and depositing it in bank. When she had saved Rs. 450, she purchased goat kids and started rearing them. When they grew up the goats were sold for Rs. 900. With this money, she purchased some utensils in the house and some jewellery for her daughter's marriage. At the Adult Education Centre, she also realized the need for limiting her family. After getting three children, she got herself operated and began to send her children to school regularly. She now looks forward to a better life and better days with confidence.

There is another case of the daughter of a rickshaw-puller, who moved forward after attending the Adult Education Centre. Her father was a liquor addict. She gradually persuaded her father to give up drinking. She had to explain to him again and again the evils of drinking and how the entire family was suffering on account of that. Finally, she succeeded. The economic position of the family started improving. Her father repaid the loan he had taken for purchase of rickshaw. The girl learned to prepare pickles which she sold in the market after completing her study in the Adult Education Centre. She had persuaded people in her village to keep their surrounding neat and clean to prevent the spread of disease.

In Tamil Nadu, in the district of Pudukottai, there was a village famous for tall grass that grows wild and can be used for making mats. Earlier all the grass from the village was being taken away by businessmen. At present, due to concerted effort of the Adult Education authorities, the women of the village have learnt to weave mats out of the local resources available. They have also established a cooperative for mat-making. This has helped the women to supplement their family income. During the night, the mat-making centre converts itself into a learning centre and the learners learn to read and write with the help of the local animator. The villagers are very confident that they are moving in the right direction and would be able to learn and also earn without depending on others.

In the coastal areas of this district, the people engaged in fishing are struggling due to competition of mechanical boats. The fishermen who go out on country crafts are not able to bring as much fish as in earlier days. During stormy days, it is not possible for them to go in the sea and have to remain idle. The RFLP in this area has tried to cover as many fishermen as possible. Apart from giving them knowledge about literacy and numeracy, the project authorities have tried to improve their functional skills by teaching them how to repair fishing nets, how to preserve fish and also about preparation of plastic wire bags. Some of these women are also working in the salt fields nearby where salt is being prepared with seawater. This is a very arduous and painstaking job, but the women are able to supplement their family income.

In the Nilgiri Hills, women labourers were being exploited by tea garden supervisors while weighing the tea leaves plucked by them. At present, the women labourers are very conscious and look at the weighing machines and calculate their wages. They have also learnt to sign the muster roll. Some of these labourers are also very enthusiastic that they will be able to bring up their children properly by giving them education and proper care. With the help of the tea garden owners, it has been possible for the Adult Education Centre to provide more recreational and cultural activities for these people. The Centres are also opening some libraries and making suitable arrangements for continuing education by persuading tea garden owners. The tea garden labourers are also interested in using their spare time for soap-making, candle-making etc., by which they can supplement their wages. The tea garden labourers have realized that literate labourers would be more productive and amenable to discipline than illiterate labourers, and so they have joined the Adult Education workers in stepping up development work among them.

Among the Paniya tribals in Tamil Nadu, for a long time, bonded labour was prevalent. The Government has taken major steps to release the bonded labourers and has arranged for their rehabilitation. In some of these villages, Adult Education Centres have been started with the help of certain social workers. They are now learning to read, write and to do some arithmetic. They are now getting used to a new life with freedom. In the district of Madhya in Karnataka, the RFLP has, with the active help and assistance of the local Mandal Panchayat, started income generation activity for the adult learners. They have also arranged for raw materials required for training the people in many skills. The women are undergoing training in the making of envelopes, soaps and detergent powder. Envelopes are in great demand for use in government offices and other stores. Soap and detergent powder, manufactured at the Adult Education Centres, are used mostly by the villagers themselves. The Mandal Panchayat has requested the local shopkeepers to promote these products in the market. Another interesting activity is chalk making in which men learners are being trained. Chalk sticks are in demand in schools as well as in the Adult Education Centres. The coloured chalk sticks, which they are also making, are used for making *rangoli* in the villages.

In the Belgaum district, the adult literacy centres for women are engaged in income generation activity such as making of agarbatti, baskets, chalk sticks and soap. The makers of these articles are also thinking in terms of forming a cooperative so that they can negotiate with large-scale purchasers. These women learners exhibit a sense of purpose and are determined to win the battle against illiteracy and social evils such as dowry, etc. They have realized that life could be much better for them than what it is today with self-reliance and support. It is this that will go a long way in fulfilling their urges and aspirations.

The *Devdasi* system is common in many states in South India. The practice of dedicating young girls in childhood to the goddess Renuka-Yallamma and their initiation into prostitution when they attain puberty has been thriving for centuries. Though the practice has been banned by the State government, it is still continuing. The main reasons for this include low levels of literacy among women, social backwardness, perpetuation of superstition and a conspiracy between the feudal castes and priests. Many of the girls dedicated to the goddess come from Scheduled castes community who are generally below the poverty line. The problem of the *Devdasi* is not only economic but also psychological. Education and better opportunities alone can help them to overcome the innumerable difficulties. Many of these girls are now joining the adult literacy classes where besides literacy and numeracy, they get training in tailoring. Other avenues of gainful employment have also been found for them so that they do not revert to their old profession.

In some other Centres of the same district, the RFLP has tried to revive folk arts and folk dances and has used it as vital medium for securing people's cooperation and community participation in adult education work. They have plans to arrange more and more cultural programmes in the villages to spread the message of literacy.

In Orisa, in a tribal village in Harichandan block, where the Bhuiya and Juan tribes live, the adult education learners have been engaged in large scale on tree plantation. Several papaya, mango, guava and some other fruit-bearing plants have been raised in the school compound and other places. The learners have also planted fruit bearing plants in their own kitchen gardens. It is hoped that this activity will help the tribal people not only in supplementing their income but also add to nutrition in their food.

In another region, in the district of Keonjhar in Orissa, where more than 80 percent of the population belongs to the Scheduled tribes, efforts have been made to open Adult Education Centres for women. All the 30 learners have been introduced to sericulture. Eleven learners have been allotted some land for engaging in *tassar* production. Asan and Arjun trees, on which the *tassar* worms are reared, have been planted by them. More and more tribal people are taking up *tassar* cultivation. With education and income generation activity, the level of these tribal people is expected to improve considerably. Literacy has been combined with *tassar* cultivation for their all-round improvement.

Voluntary Agencies, Literacy and Development

Besides the government efforts, a large number of voluntary agencies are engaged in spreading literacy. The YWCA, Madras, is using Adult Education for creating better awareness, better homes and for instilling in people a sense of confidence. Adult education means not only being able to read and write but helping each learner, and in turn, the learner's family to lead a fuller and better life with dignity and confidence. The agency has been imparting literacy skills combined with health, hygiene, childcare, family welfare and citizenship training etc. This organization has covered a wide range of women workers, maidservants, idle vendors, broom sellers, housewives and unemployed women. The YWCA functionaries had to labour a great deal to answer questions by adult women on the need for literacy at their age. At these Centres, income generation activity such as needlework, embroidery, cutting, seaming, plastic wirework, gift articles, making candles, soap and brushes, etc. are undertaken. Some Centres specialized in making candles and *agarbatti*. The past and present learners have come together on a common platform, called Adult Education Women's Progressive Forum. They take up local issues such as lack of basic amenities and other social problems for action. Group action is one of the goals of adult education campaign. Thus the YWCA has not only helped reduce illiteracy, but has also helped in fostering self-reliance for the women in the city slums.

Another effort of a similar nature has been made by Gandhi Niketan Ashram at Kulupatti near Madurai in Tamil Nadu. It has opened a number of production centres for bakery, bee keeping, match making, making of handmade paper, hand pounding of paddy, making of leather goods, soap, pottery, tanning, weaving, etc.

They have been able to link literacy with development. Gandhi Niketan has adopted a unique approach based on Gandhian concept of village development and Purna Swaraj. According to them, to realize freedom from fear is the meaning of true independence. In the Adult Education Centres, the learners learn, besides literacy and numeracy, functional skills depending upon the availability of local raw materials. They are engaged in community cleaning, tree plantation, *shramdan* activities and also get to know about health, hygiene, etc. The Centres are throbbing with activity. These are the only centres where 100 percent attendance is recorded everyday. The main idea is to enable the villagers to stand upon their own feet, settle their disputes locally and serve the weaker sections of the community with *Antodaya* spirit. In

Kalakad, in Tamilnadu, a voluntary organization, called the *'Island of Peace'*, has played an important role not only in education but in the entire development effort. Besides running the adult education centres, the organization has a network of nursery schools, women's centres, child feeding centres, palm leaf and mat making centres. All these activities are linked with adult education. Science and technology has been one of the important inputs in their programmes, whether it is an adoption of modern methods of utilizing underground resources, installation of sanitary latrines in the village, regular medical check up and making arrangements for safe drinking water. The organization has also provided for financial assistance through the formation of a Cooperative Land Mortgage Bank, irrigation cooperative, etc.

Another organization, called Vivekanand Girijan Kalyan Kendra, is doing quite useful work among the Soliga, a tribal community in the B. R. Hills. In this area opportunities for employment are very scarce. The Kendra has started making *agarbatti*, cane and bamboo handicraft, mat making, bee keeping, bakery, coir rope making, cloth weaving, carpentry, black-smithy and such other training programmes. Efforts are being made to solve the different problems faced by the tribal comunity.

Case Studies

The two case studies cited below are drawn from north Bihar where adult education work was started by the R. K. Educational Association, Bettiah, in 1979-80. Both the case studies show that participation in Adult Education Programmes has helped rural poor arouse their critical consciousness and organize themselves for concerted action.

In the month of August, 1979, the Harijans of Kurmitola, through their 'Chetna Sangh', along with Chetna Sanghs of adjoining villages, in peaceful and coordinated manner, tried to secure themselves the right to worship in a local temple of Lord Shiva. The Kurmis, who are the dominant caste of the village, did not allow the Scheduled castes to worship at the altar. The Harijans used to offer prayers from outside the sacred premises of the temple. They also participated in musical programmes arranged near the temple on festive occasions. The Scheduled castes suffer from discrimination and other social disabilities in spite of the abolition of untouchability and legal removal of the social disabilities.

Suresh Ram, a Scheduled caste youth of the village, was a regular learner at the Adult Education Centre. This helped him attain a certain level of consciousness enabling him to critically examine social disabilities suffered by the Scheduled castes in the village. He was a serious religious devotee. He used to get up early in the morning, take his bath and worship at a small shrine erected in front of his house in Harijantoli. This shrine has been established because of the inability of the Scheduled castes to worship in the main Shiva temple. In July 1979, Suresh' younger sister died of snakebite. In deep distress, the whole family left the Harijantoli and shifted to the house of Suresh's uncle, which was located near a Shiva temple. Being aware of the displeasure of the upper caste, he started offering prayers in the temple early in the morning to avoid public notice. One morning, he was somewhat late and was seen coming out from the temple by someone belonging to the Kurmi caste.

News spread in the village and the higher caste people prohibited Suresh from entering the Shiva temple. If he did this again he was to face dire consequences, he was warned. He was threatened with loss of head, if he repeated this act. However, Suresh took no notice of this threat. While the Kurmi had no objection to Scheduled castes singing *bhajans* and joining the kirtan in front of the temple, they would never concede to them the privilege of sprinkling holy water at the sacred idol of Lord Shiva. the relations between these two communities were very much strained. The Scheduled castes felt compelled to fight for the recognition of their human and constitutional rights.

Suresh narrated his experience and anguish at the meeting of the Chetna Sangh, which was specially convened for this purpose. Some leaders insisted that the demand of the Scheduled castes could not be considered, as this would vitiate the relation between the castes. However, the youths did not agree with the opinion of the elders. It was finally decided to meet the challenge posed by the Kurmis through collective action. The Scheduled castes knew that the constitution and laws were in their favour. They sought the help of agencies responsible for the abolition of the untouchability laws. The National Adult Education Project Officer advised them to see the Sub-divisional Magistrate.

A delegation thus took with them a petition explaining their grievances and mentioning the names of those Kurmis who had held out threats of violence. The delegation also met the local M.L.A., who forwarded the petition to the Superintendent of Police requesting an investigation and suitable action against the breakers of the law. The first of August 1979 was chosen by the authorities as the day for mass prayer and worship by the Scheduled castes at the Shiva temple. The decision was conveyed to the civil administration. The Chetna Sangh sought the support of the Scheduled castes living in the surrounding villages. People from all the corners started pouring in the temple premises in the early hours of the day. The Superintendent of Police apprehending breach of peace had deployed a small force to control the situation. More than 500 people gathered there in support of the Scheduled caste cause..

Contrary to expectation, the people who had issued the threat were conspicuous by their absence. They were afraid of the police and the people's support to the Scheduled castes. The *puja* took place in a state of excitement. Hundreds of people observed the Scheduled castes entering the temple and pouring holy water on the image. After this event, the police, Scheduled caste leader and other influential persons in the gathering decided that rather than taking any action against the accused Kurmis, there was the need of creating an atmosphere of brotherhood and tolerance. This would also harmonize the relation between the two communities. The temple entry was a milestone in the history of the liberation of the Scheduled castes in the locality.

This event had far-reaching importance in reordering of the existing social relationship and the social structure. The Scheduled castes, through solidarity succeeded in fighting social injustice. Awakening has come to them and they have realized their inner strength. Their participation in Adult Education Programme has helped them in reducing their feeling of powerlessness. The caste Hindus have been compelled to consider the Scheduled castes as equals so far as worship in the temples is concerned. However, they have taken this episode as challenge to their superiority. They feel that the feeling of religious equality might spill over to other sectors of activity.

The Chetna Sangh was also responsible for the mobilization of the rural poor; it has acted as a watchdog against exploitation and has helped the underprivileged and deprived section of their community to fight for better living conditions. The successful intervention of Chetna Sangh activists in the settlement of the dispute between a rich landlord and the people of Saphuatoli of Dhumnagar panchayat is a clear evidence of it. One day, Sipahi Prasad, the Adult Education Supervisor, came to this village in the morning to attend the monthly meeting of the regional Chetna Sangh. He parked his cycle near a grocery shop set up in a temporary hutment. While he was talking to other villagers, a tractor coming from the other side rammed against the temporary structure of the shop. The cycle was smashed and the shop destroyed. Sipahi and others escaped with minor injuries. The village people were very angry and they dragged the two men who caused the accident. They were abused and were about to be thrashed. Sipahi Prasad asked them to stop the beating and called for restraint. The tractor belonged to a landlord of a nearby village. It was to go to Bettiah. The person driving it was a water pump mechanic. The actual driver could not control it, thus causing the accident.

The village *chowkidar* and the *sarpanch* were contacted and the offenders were taken into custody. The tractor was seized and its owner was sent for. He however, did not turn up but sent his nephew. The village people were not prepared to talk with the nephew. The settlement could only be arrived at with the owner and the employer of the tractor driver. The Chetna Sangh leaders were determined not to go to the landlord's place. Realizing this, the landlord came to the village. Representatives from 15 villages were called and the statement of the accused was taken. They accepted the guilt but held that the offence was not deliberate. The decision was that damages had to be given to the victims. The damage to the shop was assessed at Rs. 550; the goods for sale, which were destroyed, were estimated at Rs. 150. Rs. 560 was fixed as the cost of the repair of the cycle. Rs. 40 were to be paid to the injured person for treatment.

The proceedings of the meeting were duly recorded. Compensation was to be paid then and there. As it was Sunday, the landlord promised to pay the amount on Monday. However, the people had guessed his intention, they ruled that the truck would remain in custody till the time payment was made. The landlord tried to borrow money from the Sarpanch and some other friends in the village. His prestige was thus lost under the pressure of the determined bid of the people. The friends also did not oblige. Finding no other remedy, the landlord went home and sent the money through is nephew. People were happy that they could demonstrate their solidarity and unity, which was nurtured by the Adult Education Centres through Chetna Sangh. Thus, the Adult Education Scheme was the prime mover in mobilizing the rural poor for their emancipation from the present state of social economic, physical and political disabilities.

Overview

In the multilayered societies of the Third World, struggling for modernization, literacy is one of the important inputs. The acquisition of literacy is itself a value. It enhances the self-image of a person. He rises in his own estimation as well as that of others. For the deprived and the underprivileged sections of societies, it is a tool of self-assertion and a bulwark against exploitation. Literacy promotes awareness of the inequalities in society. It creates conditions for building up solidarity of the deprived against the oppressive structure of society. It also generates the process of mobilization and prepares people for the struggle for development. In fact, literacy releases an individual from the shackles of 'unfreedom' - a term used by Dr. Amartya Sen, the Nobel Laureate - and opens up new choices for achieving a better quality of life.

The literacy programme has attracted the rural poor, Scheduled castes and tribes and women generally because the new concept of literacy is not confined to literacy and numeracy but to the creation of awareness and functionality. In most parts of the country, it has been accompanied by income generation activities which hold promise of a better life for the people and a more satisfying future.

It is, however, recognized that development requires more than education. It requires institutional change and also a change in people's attitudes. Even for these ends, the acquisition of literacy is important. In short, literacy is a necessary but not a sufficient condition for an all-round development.

References

Lal, Manohar (1986). *Role of Adult Education in Removal of Social Disabilities of* Harijans. In R. G. Singh (Ed), Depressed Classes of India : Problems and Prospects, New Delhi : B.R Publishing Corp.

Mathew, T. (1985). Adult Education and Women's Development, Ahmedabad : Sardar Patel Institute of Economic and Social Research.

Nair, P.R.G. *Decline in Birth Rate in Kerala*

Rajaih, B. (1987). Economics of Educaiton, Delhi : Mittal Publications.

Sachchidananda, *et al.* (1981). *Voluntary Efforts in Adult Education,* Patna : A.N. Sinha Institute of Social Studies.

_____(1989). Situation Analysis of the Child in Bihar, Patna: UNICEF.

Shah, S. Y. (1989). *A Source Book on Adult Education.* New Delhi : Directorate of Adult Education.

Sinha, A. (1987). A Collection of Success Stories on Adult Education, New Delhi : Directorate of Adult Education.

_____(1988). *Profiles in Literacy* : New Delhi : Directorate of Adult Education.

Subramaniam, K. V. (1977). Education and Economic Development in India, Delhi : Frank Bros. & Co.

INDEX